SUPER SUMMER LEARNING
K to GRADE 1

Dear Parents:

Summer is a great time for kids to consolidate learning in preparation for the next school year! By completing a few pages of this *Super Summer Learning* workbook each day over the summer, your child will prevent learning from sliding backward—and be well prepared to move ahead with confidence in September!

The workbook contains day-by-day review of key math and language concepts learned over the last school year, a taste of what's coming next year, plus review checklists and weekly outdoor learning activities that promote family enjoyment of the great Canadian outdoors.

We hope you and your child enjoy time together with *Super Summer Learning*.

Sincerely,

Kevin D. Misner, B.Ed. and Elaine J. Kenny, B.Ed.

Contents

© 2016 Telegraph Road, 12 Cranfield Road, Toronto, ON Canada M4B 3G8. All rights reserved. *Canadian Curriculum Press* is an imprint of Telegraph Road.

For special bulk purchases, please contact sales@canadiancurriculumpress.ca
For other inquiries, please contact inquiries@canadiancurriculumpress.ca

ISBN 978-1-4876-0168-3

Elaine J. Kenny, B.Ed. and Kevin D. Misner, B.Ed.
Senior Series Editor: Lisa Penttilä
Layout and Cover Design: Michael P. Brodey
Selected illustrations: Andrea Scobie

This material is protected by copyright. No part of it may be reproduced, stored in a retrieval system, or transmitted in any form or by any means, without prior permission in writing of Telegraph Road, nor be circulated in any other form of binding or cover other than that in which it is published and without a similar condition being imposed on the subsequent publisher.

We acknowledge the financial support of the Government of Canada through the Canada Book Fund (CBF) for our publishing activities.

 Canadian Heritage   Patrimoine canadien

Canada

Printed in Canada.

Day 1
LANGUAGE
Printing Uppercase and Lowercase Aa

Trace and print.

~~~~~~

Find blocks with uppercase 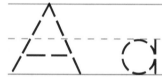. Colour them red. Find blocks with

lowercase a. Colour them yellow.

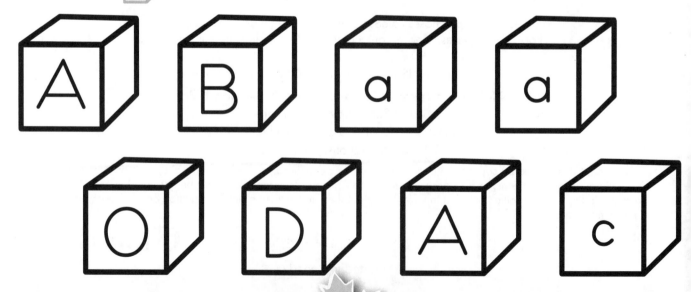

Day 1
MATH – Printing Numerals

Trace and print. Remember to start each numeral at the sky (top line) and go all the way to the ground (bottom line). Circle your best one!

FAMILY FUN ACTIVITY

Animal Rhyme Riddles

Ask your child to answer each riddle.

I live in water and my name rhymes with wish. What am I? _____

I slither and my name rhymes with lake. What am I? _____

I smell awful and my name rhymes with bunk. What am I? _____

Make up your own rhyming riddles together.

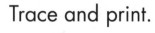

Day 2
LANGUAGE
Printing Uppercase and Lowercase Bb

Trace and print.

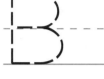

Say the name of each picture. Colour the picture if it starts with the sound of a **Bb**.

Day 2
MATH – Printing Numerals

Trace and print. Remember to start each numeral at the sky (top line) and go all the way to the ground (bottom line). Circle your best one!

✌️ **FAMILY FUN ACTIVITY**

Making Groups

Collect small items such as coins or dry macaroni. Ask your child to make a group of 3 items, and then another group of 2 items. Next move the groups together and count the total. (That makes 5!) Repeat with other groups.

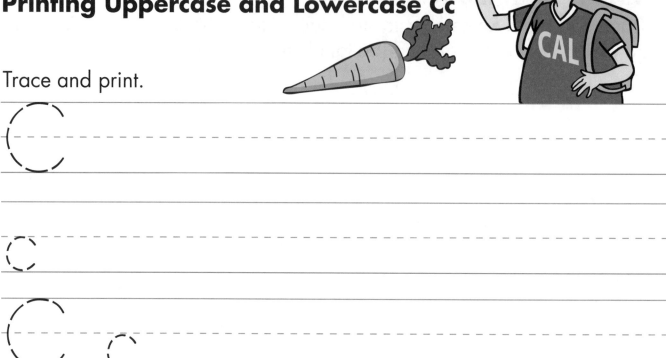

Day 3
LANGUAGE
Printing Uppercase and Lowercase Cc

Trace and print.

Add **c** to each word. Then read each word.

_at   **_ar**   **_up**

Circle every uppercase **C** and lowercase **c**. Then count them.

C E O C P D C   d e c p a c c b a

There are _____ uppercase C's and _____ lowercase c's.
.

Day 3
MATH – Printing Numerals

Trace and print. Remember to start each numeral at the top line and go all the way to the bottom line. Circle your best one!

FAMILY FUN ACTIVITY

Missing Numbers

Fill in the missing numbers. 1, 2, 3, ____ , 5, 6, ___ , 8, 9, 10

Make another sequence for your child to complete. Start with a number your child gives to you.

Day 4
LANGUAGE
Printing Uppercase and Lowercase Dd

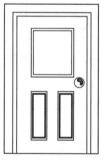

Trace and print.

Say the name of each picture. Colour each one that begins with the sound of **d**.

Add **d** to each word. Then read each word.

 _og    _rum   _uck

Day 4
MATH – Matching Numerals to Quantity

In each box draw shapes equal to the numeral.

5

8

7

3

4

6

~ FAMILY FUN ACTIVITY

Letter Hunt

Find a headline from a newspaper or magazine. Ask your child to find and circle every **d** in the headline. Try it with other letters.

Day 5
LANGUAGE
Printing Uppercase and Lowercase Ee

Trace and print.

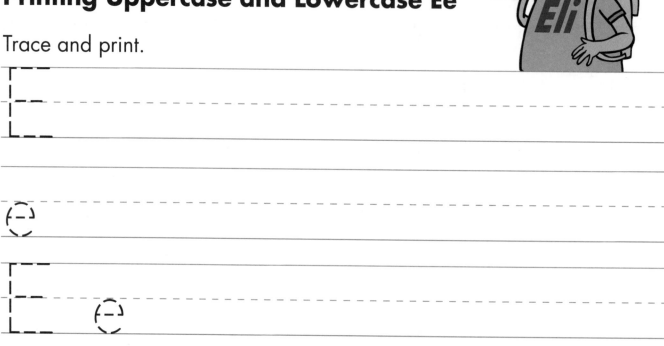

These words begin with lowercase **e**. Some have another lowercase **e** in them. Add **e** on each line. Then say each word aloud.

__gg

__y__

__ar

__raser

__lf

__l__phant

Day 5
MATH – Numerical Sequences

Print the numbers that come next on the lines. Use the numbers at the bottom of the page if you need help.

1, 2, 3, 4, 5, _____, _____, _____, 9

4, 5, 6, 7, 8, _____, _____, _____, 12

7, 8, 9, _____, _____, _____, 13

10, 11, 12, _____, _____, _____, 16

1 2 3 4 5 6 7 8 9 10 11 12 13 14 15 16 17

✋ FAMILY FUN ACTIVITY

How Many More?
Collect coins or other small objects. Make a group of 4 objects and a group of 5 objects. Ask your child to tell you which group has more. Then ask by how many more. Have fun comparing other groupings.

Ear Training
Say the words *fire, float, pig,* and *fruit.* Ask your child which word begins with a different sound than the others. Repeat with the words *pig, fish, pillow, park.*

Day 6
LANGUAGE
Printing Uppercase and Lowercase Ff

Trace and print.

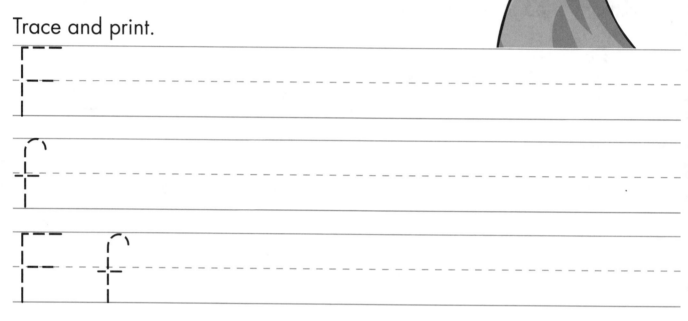

Colour the fish in the bowl. Colour the **F** fish orange. Colour the **f** fish purple. Colour the other fish any you like.

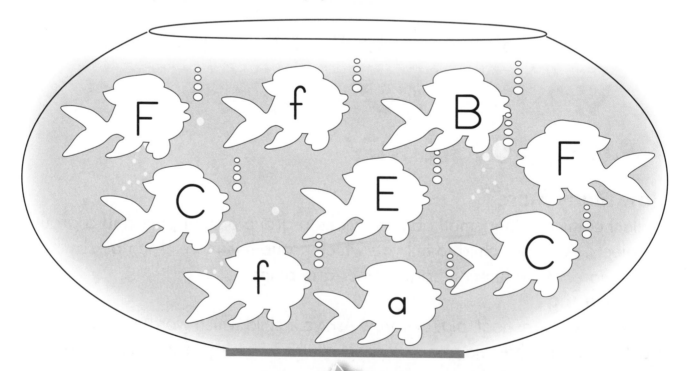

Day 6
MATH – Number Concepts

Draw and colour.

Draw 4 🍎 in the tree.

Draw 1 🚪 on the house.

Draw 3 🐦 in the tree

Draw 2 🪟 on the house.

Draw 6 🌼 around the tree.

Then colour the picture. How many objects did you draw in all? _____

👋 FAMILY FUN ACTIVITY

Fun with F

Print the letters **f** and **F**. Ask your child to name the letters. Tell her to listen for the sound of f at the beginning of *fact, fast, ferns,* and *face*. Ask your child to name other words that begin with the letter **f**.

Day 7
REVIEW

Print each letter on the line.

A

a

B

b

C

c

D

d

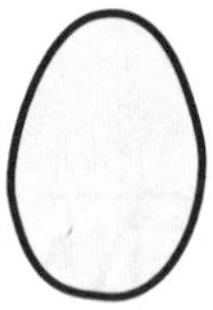

E

e

F

f

Day 7
Summer Colour by Number
Colour the picture using the colour that goes with each number.

1 Red   **2 Green**   **3 Yellow**   **4 Blue**   **5 Orange**

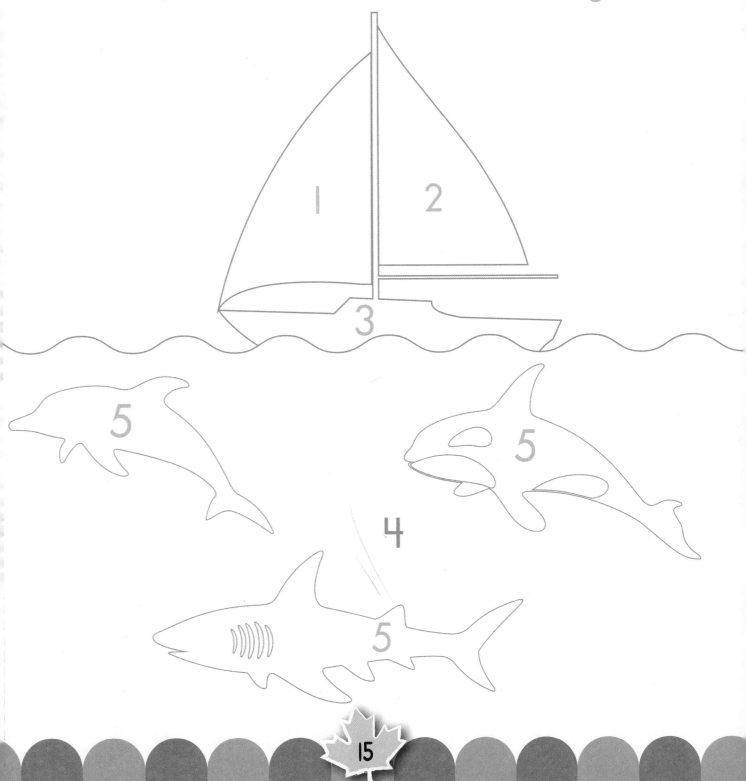

WEEK ONE

I Can Do It!
Put a checkmark beside each item you can do.

Day 1
I can print the letters **A** and **a**. .... ❑
I can print the numbers **1, 2, 3**. .... ❑

Day 2
I can print the letters **B** and **b**. .... ❑
I can print the numbers **4, 5, 6**. .... ❑

Day 3
I can print the letters **C** and **c**. .... ❑
I can print the numbers **7, 8, 9**. .... ❑

Day 4
I can print the letters **D** and **d**. .... ❑
I can draw groups of shapes. .... ❑

Day 5
I can print the letters **E** and **e**. .... ❑
I can fill out a number sequence. .... ❑

Day 6
I can print the letters **F** and **f**. .... ❑
I can follow directions. .... ❑

Day 7
I did the review page. .... ❑

Fresh Air Fun
Make Your Own Bubble Liquid

Why not make your own bubble liquid? You will need liquid dish soap (for some reason Dawn brand works best), water, glycerin (you can get this at a drug store), a pail, measuring cup, and spoon. First, pour 1.5 L (6 C) water in the pail. Add 250 ml (1 C) dish soap. Stir very gently to avoid making any bubbles. Next, add 15 ml (1 Tbsp.) glycerin. Gently stir some more until everything is completely mixed together. Cover the pail and let it stand for a few hours.

Badminton Racquet Bubbles

Try dipping an old badminton or tennis racquet (make sure it is one that no one wants to use anymore!) in the bubble liquid. Then wave it around to make dozens of tiny bubbles! Think of other things you could use to make bubbles with.

Day 1
LANGUAGE –
Printing Uppercase and Lowercase Gg

Trace and print.

G   g

g

G   g

Print **g** to complete the words. Say them aloud when you are finished.

 __oat   __ate   __lass    __rapes

 __ift    __irl

Day 1
MATH – Addition Facts
How Many Blocks?

Add. Use blocks, counters, coins, or other objects to illustrate the numbers.

$$\begin{array}{r} 2 \\ +0 \\ \hline \end{array} \qquad \begin{array}{r} 2 \\ +2 \\ \hline \end{array} \qquad \begin{array}{r} 1 \\ +1 \\ \hline \end{array} \qquad \begin{array}{r} 1 \\ +3 \\ \hline \end{array} \qquad \begin{array}{r} 2 \\ +1 \\ \hline \end{array}$$

$$\begin{array}{r} 3 \\ +2 \\ \hline \end{array} \qquad \begin{array}{r} 2 \\ +3 \\ \hline \end{array} \qquad \begin{array}{r} 1 \\ +3 \\ \hline \end{array}$$

$$\begin{array}{r} 3 \\ +1 \\ \hline \end{array} \qquad \begin{array}{r} 4 \\ +1 \\ \hline \end{array} \qquad \begin{array}{r} 4 \\ +2 \\ \hline \end{array} \qquad \begin{array}{r} 3 \\ +3 \\ \hline \end{array} \qquad \begin{array}{r} 5 \\ +1 \\ \hline \end{array}$$

FAMILY FUN ACTIVITY

Green Things
See how many green things your child can find in five minutes around the house or wherever you happen to be.

Day 2
LANGUAGE
Printing Uppercase and Lowercase Hh

Trace and print.

Circle every uppercase **H**.

E F H A

H B H

Circle every lowercase **h**.

h f e h

d a b

Colour to find the hidden picture!
Use green to colour the spaces with
H in them. Use red to the spaces
with **h** in them.

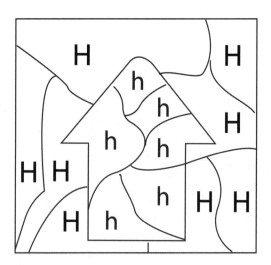

Day 2
MATH – Measurement

Rulers are used to measure things. This ruler measures 18 centimetres (cm). How many centimetres long do you think each pencil is? Use the ruler to find out. Put your answer in the box.

| 1cm | 2 | 3 | 4 | 5 | 6 | 7 | 8 | 9 | 10 | 11 | 12 | 13 | 14 | 15 | 16 | 17 | 18 |

cm

cm

cm

cm

cm

cm

cm

Day 3
LANGUAGE
Printing Uppercase and Lowercase Ii

Ike

Trace and print.

I

i

I i

Circle these **Ii** word in the puzzle.

n	e	c	l	m	t	r	c	l
i	i	i	s	i	m	n	t	a
i	i	l	i	n	s	e	c	t
e	r	l	l	k	i	i	c	n
c	i	c	e	c	r	e	a	m
t	k	i	m	p	m	n	n	i
e	i	r	r	i	t	t	s	l

ill

insect

imp

ink

it

ice cream

Day 3
MATH – Measurement

Measuring with a ruler is fun! Draw a pencil long enough to match the number of centimetres (cm) shown.

1cm	2	3	4	5	6	7	8	9	10	11	12	13	14	15	16	17	18

6 cm

3 cm

9 cm

15 cm

7 cm

11 cm

Colour the **longest** pencil red.
Colour the **shortest** pencil blue.

FAMILY FUN ACTIVITY

My Letter Book
Help your child print the letters **i** and **I** at the top of a piece of paper. Look for words that start with **i** or **I** in a magazine or newspaper. Ask your child to cut out and paste the words onto the page. Do the same on separate pages for **Jj** and **Kk**.

Day 4
LANGUAGE
Printing Uppercase and Lowercase Jj

Trace and print.

Say the name of each picture. Colour each one that begins with the sound of **j**.

Day 4
MATH – Counting by Twos

Count by 2's to find out how many shoes there are. Write the number below each pair as you count.

___ ___   ___   ___   ___   ___   ___   ___   ___   ___

Count out loud:

2, 4, 6, 8, 10, 12, 14, 16, 18, 20!

✋ FAMILY FUN ACTIVITY

Continue the Story
Start a story with the sentence below and then ask your child continue it. "One day when I was paddling my kayak down a river…. "

WEEK TWO

Day 5
LANGUAGE
Printing Uppercase and Lowercase Kk

Trace and print.

These words start with lowercase **k**. Print lowercase **k** on the lines. Read the words aloud.

_ey   _ite   _itten

This name has two uppercase **K**s in it. Print uppercase **K** on the lines. Read the name aloud.

_ing _ong

26

Day 5
MATH – Counting by Fives

Counting by 5's is fun! Count aloud by 5's to find out how many fingers there are. Print the numbers on the lines.

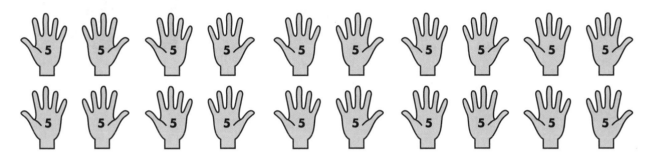

— — — — — — — — — — — — — — — — — — — —

— — — — — — — — — —

 **5, 10, 15, 20, 25, 30, 35, 40, 45, 50, 55, 60, 65, 70, 75, 80, 85, 90, 95, 100!**

FAMILY FUN ACTIVITY

Bigger or Smaller?
Ask your child to name 6 things in the kitchen that are bigger than a cereal box and 6 things that are smaller.

Day 5
LANGUAGE
Printing Uppercase and Lowercase Ll

Trace and print.

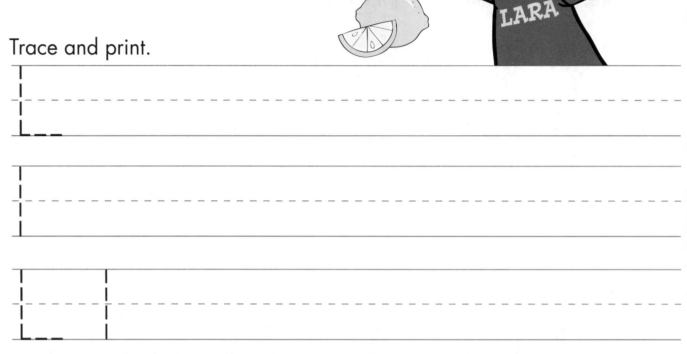

Use blue to colour the luggage with uppercase **L** on it. Use red to colour the luggage with a lowercase **l** on it.

Day 6
MATH
Counting by Tens

Count aloud by 10's to find out how many coins there are. Print the numbers on the lines.

_____ _____ _____ _____ _____

_____ _____ _____ _____ _____

FAMILY FUN ACTIVITY

My Letter Book

Help your child print the letters **L** and **I** at the top of a piece of paper. Then, using a page from a magazine or newspaper, have her cut out and paste all the words that start with **L** or **I** on the page.

Day 7
REVIEW
Print each letter on the line.

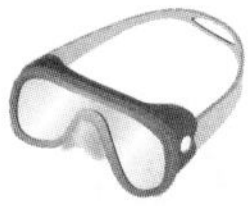

G

g

H

h

I

i

J

j

K

k

L

l

Day 7
REVIEW

Count by 2's and 5's to find the number of lilypads between each frog and his friends.

WEEK TWO

I Can Do It!

Put a checkmark beside each item you can do.

Day 1

I can print the letters **G** and **g**......................... ❏

I know some basic addition. .... ❏

Day 2

I can print the letters **H** and **h**. .... ❏

I can use a ruler. .... ❏

Day 3

I can print the letters **I** and **i**. .... ❏

I can measure new things. .... ❏

Day 4

I can print the letters **J** and **j**. .... ❏

I can count twos. .... ❏

Day 5

I can print the letters **K** and **k**. .... ❏

I can count by 5's. .... ❏

Day 6

I can print the letters **L** and **l**. .... ❏

I can count by 10's. .... ❏

Day 7

I reviewed this week's letters. .... ❏

Fresh Air Fun

Pebble Math

Have fun outside! Use pebbles to practise skip counting.

Go for a walk with a friend and collect enough pebbles to fill a yogurt or similar container. Find a flat outdoor area to pour out the pebbles. Count by 2's to find out how many pebbles you have all together. Ask a partner to take away some pebbles while you hide your eyes. Count by 2's again to find out how many you have left. Then, put them all back in the container.

Repeat a few times. Ask your partner to take away a different number of pebbles each time. Don't peek! Then repeat and count by 5's to find out how many are left.

Next, trade places with your partner so you take away pebbles and your partner counts by 2's and 5's. Then put the pebbles back in the container, put the lid on it, and set them aside for another day!

Day 1
LANGUAGE

Printing Uppercase and Lowercase Mm

Trace and print.

M

m

M m

Circle pictures of things that start with the **Mm** sound.

WEEK THREE

Day 1
MATH – Counting by Threes

Count by 3's to find the number of blades on the windmills. Write the numbers on the lines as you count.

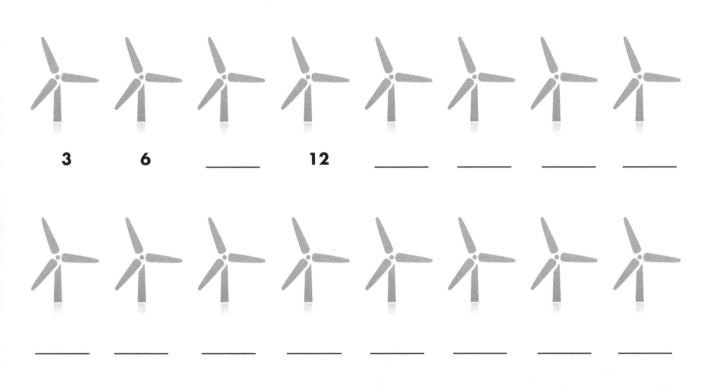

3   6   ____   12   ____   ____   ____   ____

____   ____   ____   ____   ____   ____   ____   ____

✋ FAMILY FUN ACTIVITY

Make a group of 6 small items such as dry macaroni or coins. Ask your child to make a group that has 2 more than 6 in it. Next, ask him to make a group with 2 fewer than 6 in it. Talk about other examples of more than and less than.

35

Day 2
LANGUAGE

Printing Uppercase and Lowercase Nn

Trace and print.

Add **n** and read each word.

_est

_ut

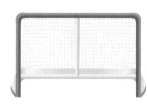

_et

Circle every uppercase **N** and lowercase **n**.

M N L I J N K B N M

l m a n j n b c b n

WEEK THREE

Day 2
MATH – Counting by Fives using Money

Count the nickels. Write the total amount in the blank at the end of each row. Example:

          <u>15</u>¢

          ____¢

          ____¢

          ____¢

Bonus: How many nickels does it take to make 50¢? _____

✋FAMILY FUN ACTIVITY

Fun with Opposites

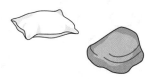

Try playing the opposite game with your child. Ask her to do the **opposite** of the following instructions.

Sit down.   **Frown.**   **Say goodbye.**   **Open your eyes.**

Day 3
LANGUAGE

Printing Uppercase and Lowercase Oo

Trace and print.

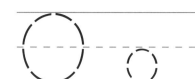

Use **red** to colour the spaces with Oo. Colour the other spaces **blue**.

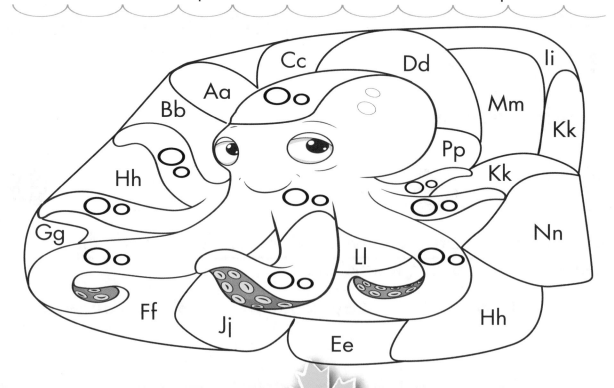

Day 3
MATH – Counting by Tens using Dimes

Count the dimes. Write the total amount in the blank at the end of each row.

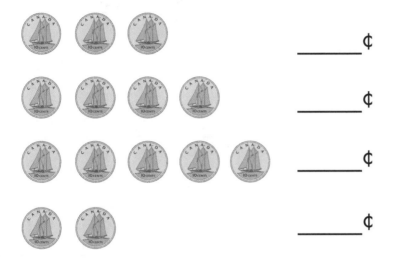

_____ ¢

_____ ¢

_____ ¢

_____ ¢

Bonus: How many dimes does it take to make $1? _____
Hint: $1 is the same as 100¢.

✋ FAMILY FUN ACTIVITY

Our Family Order

Help your child name family members or special friends from youngest to oldest. Write their names on a piece of paper for your child.

Day 4
LANGUAGE
Printing Uppercase and Lowercase Pp

Trace and print.

P

p

P

p

Colour all the objects that begin with the sound of **Pp**, as in **pizza**.
Colour the pepperoni on the pizza **red**. Then colour the rest of the pizza.

Day 4
MATH – Number Recognition

Play this game with an adult. Have the adult call out a number. Then find that number and point to it. Then switch roles: you call out the number and as the adult to point to it. Who is the fastest?

1	2	3	4	5	6	7	8	9	10
11	12	13	14	15	16	17	18	19	20
21	22	23	24	25	26	27	28	29	30
31	32	33	34	35	36	37	38	39	40
41	42	43	44	45	46	47	48	49	50
51	52	53	54	55	56	57	58	59	60
61	62	63	64	65	66	67	68	69	70
71	72	73	74	75	76	77	78	79	80
81	82	83	84	85	86	87	88	89	90
91	92	93	94	95	96	97	98	99	100

FAMILY FUN ACTIVITY

P, Please!

Print the letters **P** and **p**. Ask your child to identify which is uppercase and which is lowercase. Tell him to listen closely for the sound of *p* at the beginning of *Peter, pig, pepper, peanut,* and *put*. Next, ask him to name other words that begin with *p*.

Day 5
LANGUAGE
Printing Uppercase and Lowercase Qq

Trace and print.

Trace the uppercase **Q** or lowercase **q** on each line. Colour the picture.

Queen Quinn
is
quite quiet.

42

WEEK THREE

Day 5
MATH – Writing Numbers

Fill in the missing numbers.

1　2　3　___ ___ ___ ___ ___ ___ 10

11 ___ 13　___ ___ ___ ___ ___ ___ ___

21 ___ ___ ___ 25 ___ ___ ___ 29 ___

___ 32 ___ ___ ___ ___ 37 ___ ___ ___

41 ___ 43　___ ___ ___ ___ ___ ___ ___

51 ___ ___ 54 ___ ___ ___ 58 ___ ___

___ 62 ___ ___ 65 ___ ___ ___ 69 ___

___ ___ 73 ___ ___ 76 ___ ___ ___ ___

___ ___ ___ ___ ___ ___ 87 ___ ___ ___

___ ___ 93 ___ ___ ___ ___ 98 ___ ___

You did it!

🖐 FAMILY FUN ACTIVITY

Ask your child to think about the following math problem.
Diya read 5 books in January and 3 books in February. How many books did he read altogether?
Ask your child make up a similar word problem for you to solve.

Day 6
LANGUAGE
Printing Uppercase and Lowercase Rr

Trace and print.

R

r

R r

Circle every **R** and every **r**.

r r B r R F J r R K I M R

There are ___ R's and ___ r's.

Circle the pictures that start with the sound of **Rr**.

44

Day 6
MATH – Roll and Colour

Collect 6 differently coloured crayons and one die. Roll the die. Using any colour you like, colour the section of the rainbow that includes that number. Continue rolling and colouring each section using a different colour for each section. Roll again if the same number comes up again.

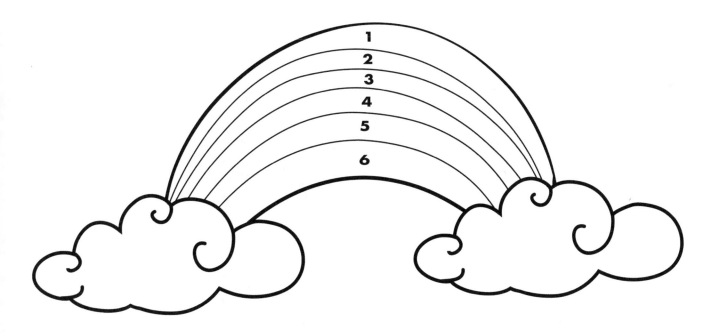

FAMILY FUN ACTIVITY

Toy Stories

Talk about your child's favourite toy. Ask your child to make up a story about something that might happen if that toy came to life. What would the toy do? Where would it go? What would your child say to the living toy?

Day 7
REVIEW

Print each letter on the line.

WEEK THREE

I Can Do It!
Put a checkmark beside each item you can do.

Day 1
I can print the letters **M** and **m**. ....☐
I can count by 3's...☐

Day 2
I can print the letters **N** and **n**. ....☐
I can count using nickels. ....☐

Day 3
I can print the letters **O** and **o**. ....☐
I can count using dimes. ....☐

Day 4
I can print the letters **P** and **p**. ....☐
I can recognize 1-100...☐

Day 5
I can print the letters **Q** and **q**. ....☐
I know the numbers from 1-100. ....☐

Day 6
I can print the letters **R** and **r**. ....☐
I know the numbers on a die. ....☐

Day 7
I did the letter review. ....☐

Fresh Air Fun
Record a Memory

Use a tape recorder or smart phone to record an adult telling about something cute you did when you were little. Play the recording back later and listen carefully. Then write down the story. Draw a picture to match. Put up your writing and picture where you can enjoy it.

_____

_____

_____

Day 1
LANGUAGE
Printing Uppercase and Lowercase Ss

Trace and print.

Colour the uppercase **S** snakes purple. Colour the lowercase snakes yellow.

WEEK FOUR

Day 1
MATH – More or Less

Circle the number that means **more** in in each box.

25 **14**	**26** **17**	**71** **72**	**88** **65**

9 **12**	**18** **71**	**3** **9**	**59** **60**

Circle the number that means **less** in each box.

53 **35**	**21** **12**	**40** **60**	**29** **41**

38 **27**	**13** **31**	**92** **94**	**45** **54**

FAMILY FUN ACTIVITY

My Letter Book

Help your child print **S** and **s** at the top of a piece of paper. Then look for words that start with **S** or **s** in a magazine or newspaper. Ask him to cut out and paste the words onto the page. Do the same for **V** and **W**.

Day 2
LANGUAGE
Printing Uppercase and Lowercase Tt

Trace and print.

Draw three pictures of things that start with **Tt** sound.

Day 2
MATH – Word Problems

Samantha counted 4 trees in her front yard. She then counted 2 trees in backyard. How many trees were there altogether?

● ● ● ● + ○ ○ = ☐

Make up your own word problems based on these counters. Can an adult solve your math problems?

● ● ●

_____

○ ○ ○

_____

● ● ●

_____

✋ FAMILY FUN ACTIVITY

Animal Homes

Ask your child to draw the different kinds of animals who live in trees. Then next time you are outside with your child, look for a bird nest, squirrel nest or other animal homes.

WEEK FOUR

Day 3
LANGUAGE
Printing Uppercase and Lowercase Uu

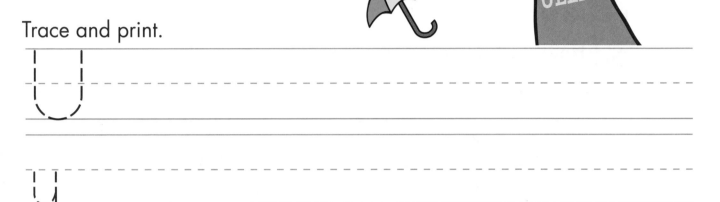

Trace and print.

Colour all the uppercase **U**'s yellow and all the lowercase **u**'s blue.

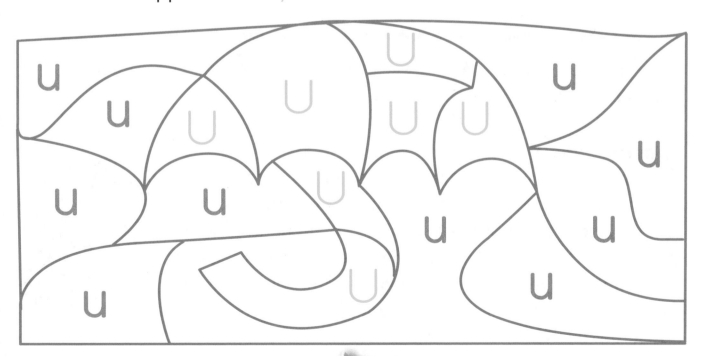

Day 3
MATH – Tally Charts

Ridwan went to a petting zoo and saw four donkeys, ten pigs, and eight sheep. He made a tally chart of the animals he saw. Can you help him finish the chart?

Bonus How many animals were there altogether? [   ]

~~~~~~

✋ FAMILY FUN ACTIVITY

Good Friends
Talk with your child about friendship. Together, come up with three ways to be a good friend. (Some ideas are to offer to share a toy or treat, to invite someone to play a game, and to show interest in the other person by asking questions.) Have your child practice asking questions that he might ask a new friend (for example, what is your favourite food?).

Day 4
LANGUAGE
Printing Uppercase and Lowercase Vv

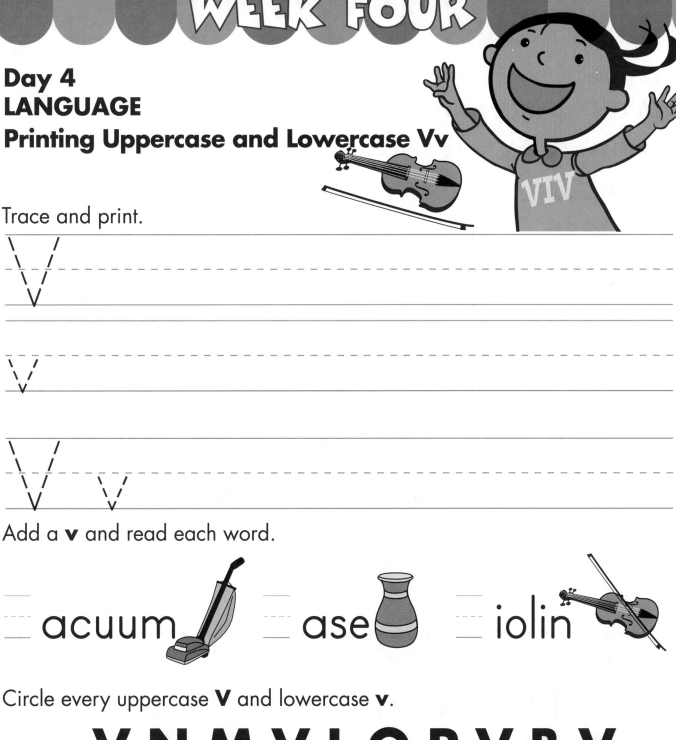

Trace and print.

Add a **v** and read each word.

_ acuum   _ ase   _ iolin

Circle every uppercase **V** and lowercase **v**.

V N M V L O P V B V
n u v v e c b a v m

There are ____ uppercase **V**'s and ____ lowercase **v**'s

Day 4
MATH – Bar Graphs

Jasmine made a graph of her friends' favourite foods.

Favourite Foods

Pizza   Vegetables   Cereal   Fruit

How many friends like pizza most? _____

How many friends like cereal most? _____

How many more friends like pizza than like fruit? _____

FAMILY FUN ACTIVITY

TV Favourite

Have your child draw a picture of a favourite TV character. When finished, ask for two or three reasons why this character is a favourite.

Day 5
LANGUAGE
Printing Uppercase and Lowercase Ww

Trace and print.

Draw three pictures of things that start with **Ww** sound.

Day 5
MATH—Squares

A square has four sides that are all the same length ☐.

Help Pat Beaver find the way home. Colour the path that has only squares ☐.

Day 6
LANGUAGE
Printing Uppercase and Lowercase Xx

Trace and print.

X
X
X   x

Add **x** and read each word.

bo_

fo_

e_it

_-ray

_ylophone

Day 6
MATH – Squares

Colour the squares blue. Put an **X** on shapes that are not square.

~~~~~~

FAMILY FUN ACTIVITY

Shorter or Longer?
Place a pencil on a table. Ask your child to look around the room and name five things that are longer than the pencil and five things that are shorter than the pencil.

Day 7
REVIEW

Print each letter on the line.

I Can Do It!

Put a checkmark beside each item you can do.

Day 1

I can print the letters **S** and **s**. .... ❏

I can compare numbers. .... ❏

Day 2

I can print the letters **T** and **t**. .... ❏

I can solve word problems. .... ❏

Day 3

I can print the letters **U** and **u**. .... ❏

I can create a tally chart. .... ❏

Day 4

I can print the letters **V** and **v**. .... ❏

I can read a bar graph. .... ❏

Day 5

I can print the letters **W** and **w**. .... ❏

I can recognize squares. .... ❏

Day 6

I can print the letters **X** and **x**. .... ❏

I know my shapes. .... ❏

Day 7

I did the letter review. .... ❏

Fresh Air Fun
Your Name Rocks!

Have fun outside! Paint the letters of your name on some smooth stones. Then use them to decorate a window sill, big flower pot, or corner of a garden.

You will need acrylic paints, brushes, and a bottle of clear nail polish OR several bottles of nail polish in your favourite colours, and lots of big and small smooth stones. You may also want a container to store your things in so you can use them another time.

Paint outside where you can put down newspaper to catch spills, and wear something you don't mind getting drips on. Paint each letter of your name on one smooth stone. Don't forget the first letter of your name needs to be an uppercase letter! Let the paint dry. Paint a top coat of clear nail polish on them to make them waterproof. Let dry. Arrange the stones to spell your name in a big flower pot, on a window sill, or somewhere else you can admire your work.

More ideas:

1. Paint one uppercase alphabet and one lowercase alphabet. (That's 52 stones!) Arrange the lowercase letters in alphabetical order. Then match an uppercase letter to each one.

2. Paint stones to spell out a surprise birthday message for someone special. Paint an exclamation mark (!) to put at the end of the message. Then put the message somewhere the person will see it.

Once you start, you will probably want to do more rock painting! Save your supplies in a bin with a lid so it's ready for next time.

Day 1
LANGUAGE – Printing Uppercase and Lowercase Yy

Trace and print.

Add **y** and read each word.

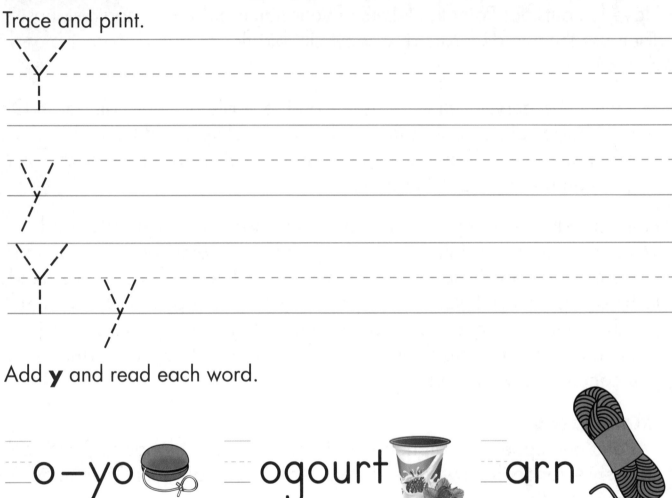

__o-yo☺   __ogourt   __arn

Circle the **y** in these words:

yard   yes   yellow   yam   yell

Day 1
MATH - Triangles

Triangles have 3 sides and 3 corners.
Trace each triangle with blue. Put a red dot on each corner.

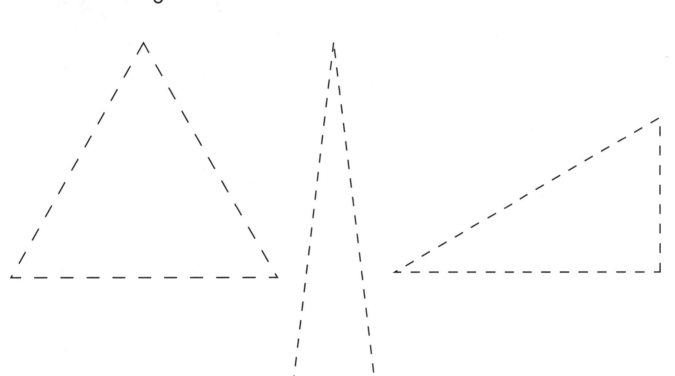

🖐 FAMILY FUN ACTIVITY

Orange as an Orange

How many orange things can you and your child name in two minutes?
Work together to come up with as many as you can. Let your child watch
you use tally marks to keep track of the number. Then try again with another colour and let your child draw the tally marks to keep track.

Day 2
LANGUAGE – Printing Uppercase and Lowercase Zz

Trace and print.

Z

Z

Z z

Colour all of the pictures that begin with the sound of **Z**.

Day 2
MATH – Rectangles

All rectangles have 4 sides, but only the opposite sides are the same length. Colour the rectangles.

Circle the rectangles in the following pictures.

FAMILY FUN ACTIVITY
Family Favourites

Work together to make a special family recipe with your child.

Day 3
LANGUAGE – Printing Lowercase Letters Review

Trace the letters. Add the missing lowercase letters.

a b c _____ _____ _____

g _____ _____ _____ _____ _____ i _____

n _____ _____ _____ _____ _____ t

u _____ _____ _____ _____ z

Day 3
LANGUAGE – Printing Uppercase Letters Review

Trace the letters. Add the missing uppercase letters.

A _____ F

G _____ L

M _____ O

R _____

W _____ Z

Day 4
LANGUAGE – Uppercase and Lowercase Letter Match

Draw lines to connect the matching uppercase and lowercase letters.

A B C D E F

d a f b c e

G H I J K L M

i g h m k l j

Day 4
LANGUAGE – Uppercase and Lowercase Letter Match

Draw lines to connect the matching uppercase and lowercase letters.

N O P Q R S T

r n t s q o p

U V W X Y Z

v w u z x y

Day 5
LANGUAGE – Beginning Letter Sounds

Say the name of each picture. Print the letter you hear at the beginning of the word.

Day 5
LANGUAGE – Beginning Letter Sounds

Say the name of each picture. Print the letter you hear at the beginning of the word.

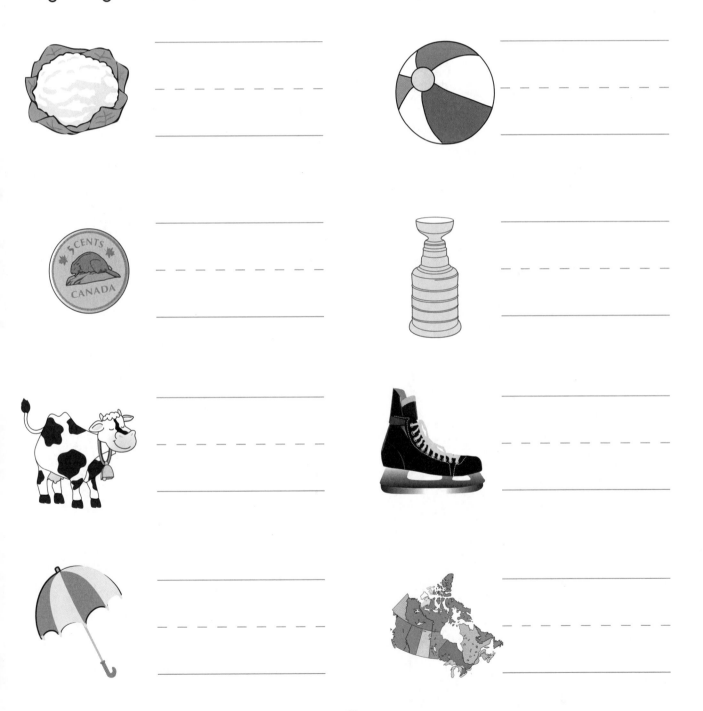

Day 6
LANGUAGE – Trace and Match Lowercase to Uppercase Letters

Trace each letter. Draw lines to connect matching lowercase and uppercase letters.

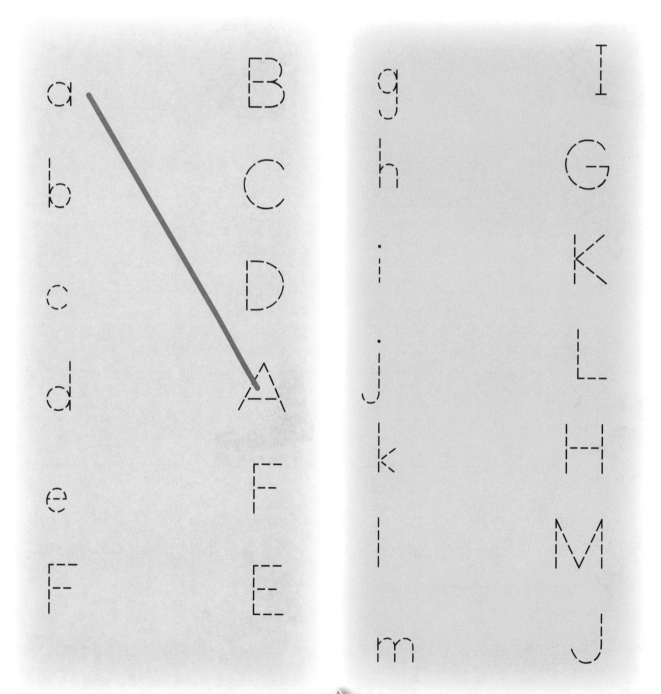

Day 6
LANGUAGE – Trace and Match Lowercase to Uppercase Letters

Trace each letter. Draw lines to connect matching lowercase and uppercase letters.

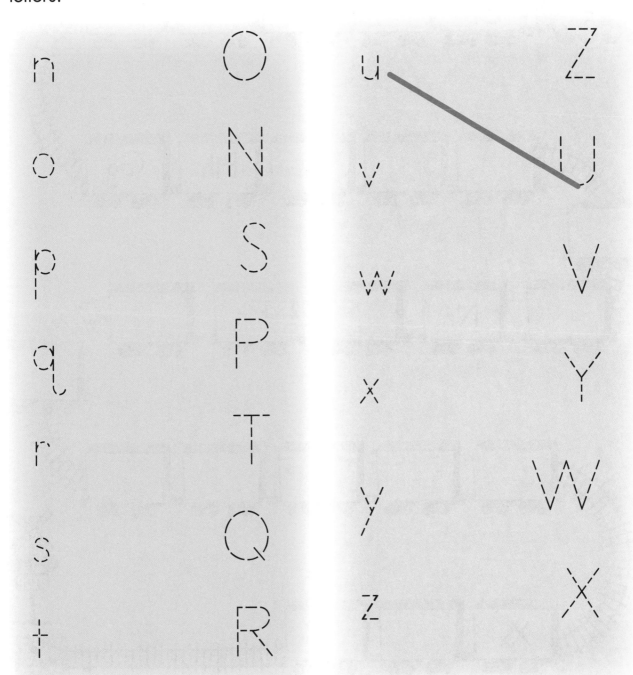

Day 7
Review

Fill in the missing letters on the alphabet train.

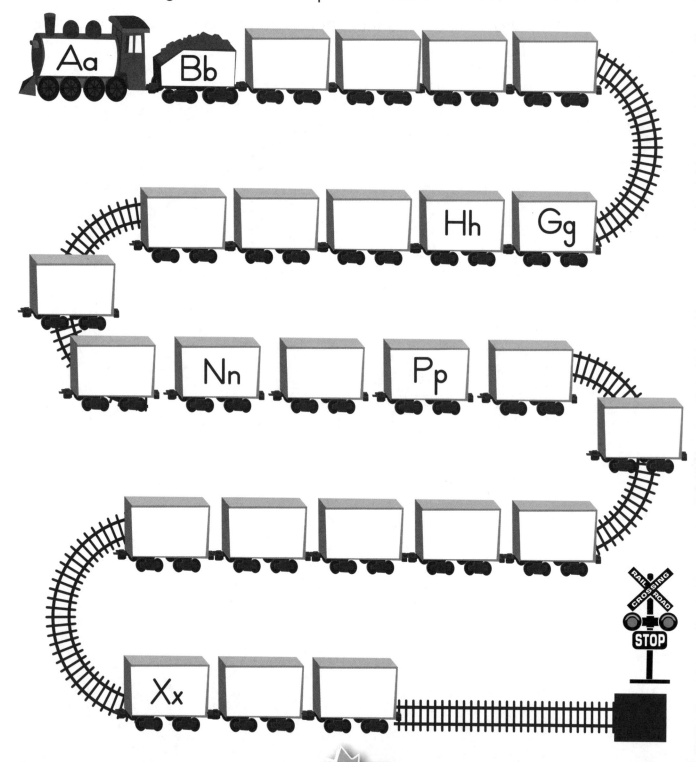

Day 7
Review - Shapes

Colour the rectangles yellow. Colour the squares **green**. Colour the triangles **red**. Draw a smiling face on the circle.

I Can Do It!

Put a checkmark beside each item you can do.

Day 1

I can print the letters **Y** and **y**. .... ❏
I know about triangles. .... ❏

Day 2

I can print the letters **Z** and **z**. .... ❏
I know about rectangles. .... ❏

Day 3

I can print lowercase letters.. .... ❏
I can print uppercase letters. .... ❏

Day 4

I can print the letters **V** and **v**. .... ❏
I can read a bar graph. .... ❏

Day 5

I can match uppercase to lowercase letters. .... ❏
I can print beginning letter sounds. .... ❏

Day 6

I can match lowercase to uppercase letters. .... ❏

Day 7

I did the alphabet review. .... ❏
I did the shape review. .... ❏

Fresh Air Fun
Letter and Shape Search

Have fun outside! Go outside and look for things that have this week's letters in them. Put a checkmark beside each letter when you find something.

Yy_____

Zz_____

Look for something outside that is a rectangle. Draw a picture of it here.

Look for something outside that is a triangle. Draw a picture of it here.

Day 1
LANGUAGE, THINKING

Draw a picture of yourself. Colour your picture. Fill in the blanks.

My name is

_____

_____.

I am _____

years old. I live in Canada.

Colour the Canadian flag.

Day 1
LANGUAGE, THINKING - Following Directions

Follow the directions.

Here is Dad.
Colour his pants blue.
Draw 3 buttons on his shirt.

Here is a bus.
Colour it yellow.
Draw 4 windows on it.

Here is a snake.
Draw stripes on it.
Colour the stripes purple.

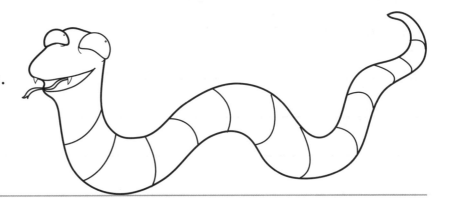

Day 2
LANGUAGE, THINKING

Draw a picture of your family. Colour your picture. Fill in the blanks.

There are _____ people in my family.

These are their names.

_____

_____

_____

_____

Day 2
LANGUAGE – Following Directions

Follow the directions.

Here is a bowl.
Draw a yellow banana in it.
Colour the bowl green.

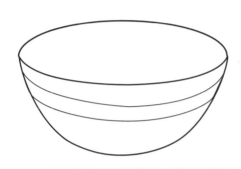

Here is a pail and sandcastle.
Colour the pail blue.
Draw a flag on each tower.
Colour them red.

Here is a pizza.
Draw 6 pepperoni slices on it.
Draw lines to divide it into 4 pieces.

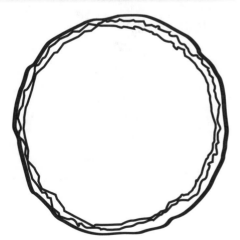

Day 3
LANGUAGE – Noticing Details

Read the story with an adult. Fill in the blanks with words from the story.

> Sarah and Bradley have a dog. Their dog's name is Buddy. Buddy is a boy dog. Buddy loves going on walks.

Sarah and Bradley have a _____.

Their dog's name is _____.

Buddy loves going on _____.

Day 3
LANGUAGE – Noticing Details - Sorting

Sort the objects. Circle the one that is different.

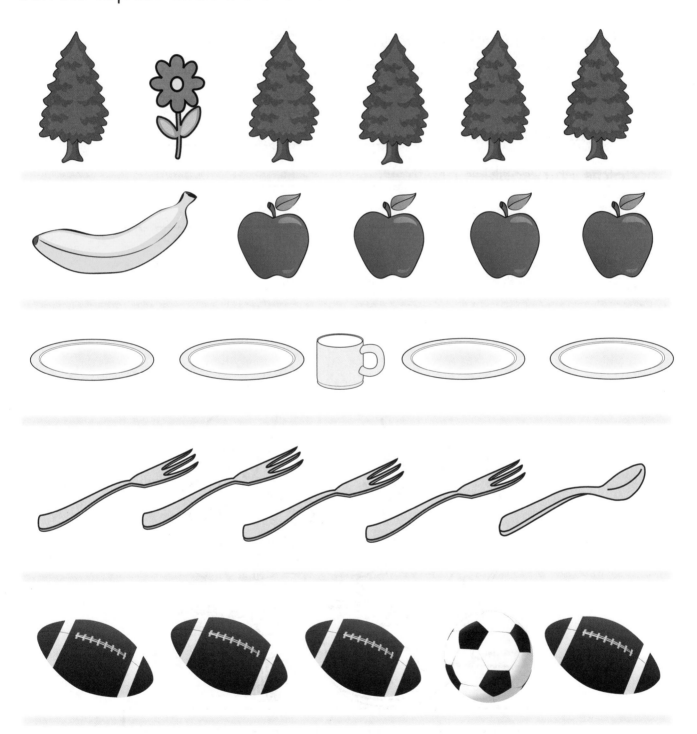

Day 4
LANGUAGE – Noticing Details, Reading for Meaning

Read the story. Fill in the blanks with words from the story.

Francis and Michele love to bake. Chocolate chip cookies are their favourite. They also bake delicious banana muffins.

Francis and Michele love to _____.

Chocolate chip cookies are their _____.

They also make delicious _____.

Day 4
LANGUAGE – Noticing Details - Sorting

Sort the objects. Draw an X on the one that doesn't belong.

Sort the flowers. Colour the daisies pink. Colour the tulips

 yellow. Colour the roses  red.

Day 5
MATH – Ordinal Numbers

Print the ordinal number words in the correct order.

second	ninth	third	tenth	fifth
first	seventh	fourth	sixth	eighth

1st _____

2nd _____

3rd _____

4th _____

5th _____

6th _____

7th _____

8th _____

9th _____

10th _____

Day 5
MATH – Following Instructions, Ordinal Numbers

Read each ordinal number. Draw the matching shape in the box.

 1st   **2nd**   **3rd**   **4th**   **5th**   **6th**

second		fifth

first		sixth

fourth		third

Day 6
MATH – Graphing, Counting, Ordinal Numbers

Colour boxes to match the number of apples in each tree. Then answer the questions.

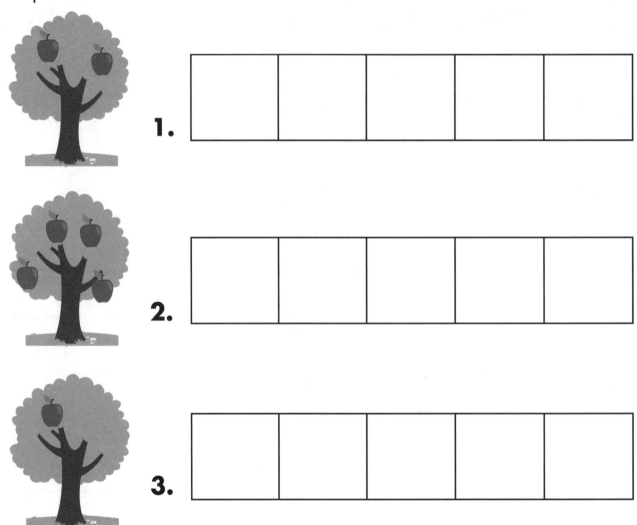

1.

2.

3.

How many apples are in the first tree? _____

How many apples are in the second tree? _____

How many apples are in the third tree? _____

Day 6
MATH – Graphing, Counting

Count each type of fruit. Complete the graph to match. The apples have been done for you. Then answer the questions.

Fruit in a Bowl
Each picture equals one fruit.

Which fruit is there the most of? _____

Which fruit is there the fewest of? _____

Which two fruit are there equal numbers of? _____

Day 7
Review - Ordinal Numbers

Print the matching ordinal numbers on the lines.

1st _____   6th _____

2nd _____   7th _____

3rd _____   8th _____

4th _____   9th _____

5th _____   10th _____

tenth
first
third
fourth
seventh
ninth
eighth
fifth
sixth
second

Day 7
Review

Colour the first bead **red**.
Colour the third bead **green**.
Colour the seventh bead **yellow**.
Colour the fourth bead **blue**.
Colour the second bead **purple**.
Colour the fifth bead **pink**.
Colour the eighth bead **black**.
Colour the sixth bead **orange**.
Colour the ninth bead **brown**.
Colour the tenth bead **grey**.

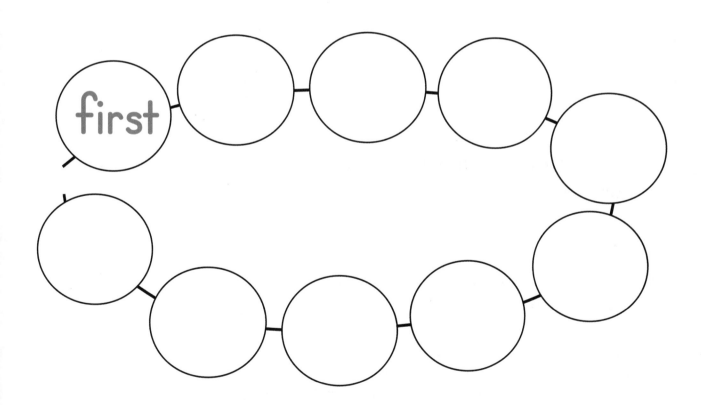

WEEK SIX

I Can Do It!
Put a checkmark beside each item you can do.

Day 1
I can tell all about me. .... ❑
I can follow directions. .... ❑

Day 2
I can tell about my family. .... ❑
I can follow directions. .... ❑

Day 3
I notice details. .... ❑
I notice something different. .... ❑

Day 4
I notice details. .... ❑
I notice something that doesn't belong. .... ❑

Day 5
I can print ordinal numbers. .... ❑
I can use ordinal numbers. .... ❑

Day 6
I can complete a graph. .... ❑
I can read a graph. .... ❑

Day 7
I reviewed colour words and ordinal numbers. .... ❑

Fresh Air Fun
Make a Leaf Collection

Have fun outside! Collect 5 different kinds of leaves. (Ask an adult for permission first.) Sort them from biggest to smallest. Which leaf has smooth edges? Which leaf is the darkest colour?
Draw the five leaves here.

Day 1
LANGUAGE - Colour Words

Print the colour word under each can of paint. Use the word list on the opposite page to help.

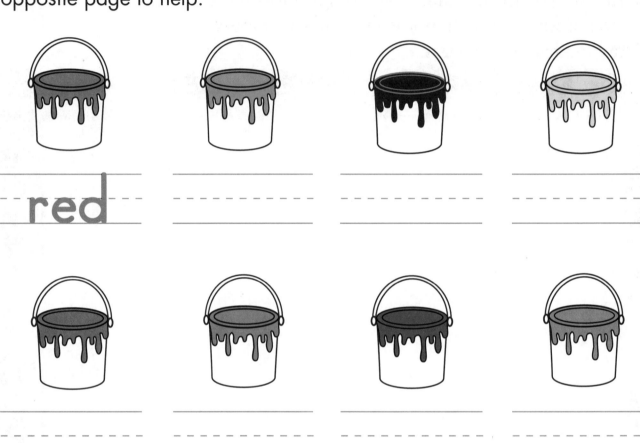

red

Day 1
Colour Word Search

Find the colour words in the puzzle.

```
a b l a c k d e
r e d o p i n k
p u r p l e l d
y e y e l l o w
o f o r a n g e
a b r o w n a p
t a g r e e n r
g r e y b l u e
```

black	green	purple
blue	grey	red
brown	orange	yellow
	pink	

Day 2
LANGUAGE - Word Scramble

Unscramble the letters. Print the word on the line.

koob

_____

- - - - - - - - - - - - -

_____

acr

_____

- - - - - - - - - - - - -

_____

upc

_____

- - - - - - - - - - - - -

_____

kibe

_____

- - - - - - - - - - - - -

_____

eetr

_____

- - - - - - - - - - - - -

_____

eflwor

_____

- - - - - - - - - - - - -

_____

ohsue

_____

- - - - - - - - - - - - -

_____

kcurt

_____

- - - - - - - - - - - - -

_____

tasr

_____

- - - - - - - - - - - - -

_____

Day 2
LANGUAGE – Colour Scramble

Think of your favourite colour. Print the letters of the colour word in scrambled order on the line. Ask someone to guess the scrambled word. Then colour the paint can in that colour.

Day 3
LANGUAGE – Words I Know

Make a dictionary! Print your name beside the letter it starts with. Think of words you know that start with other letters. Print them on the matching lines.

Aa

Bb

Cc

Dd

Ee

Ff

Day 3
LANGUAGE – Words I Know

Make a dictionary! Print your name beside the letter it starts with. Think of words you know that start with other letters. Print them on the matching lines.

Gg

Hh

Ii

Jj

Kk

Ll

Day 4
LANGUAGE – Words I Know

Make a dictionary! Print your name beside the letter it starts with. Think of words you know that start with other letters. Print them on the matching lines.

Mm

Nn

Oo

Pp

Qq

Rr

Ss

Day 4
LANGUAGE – Words I Know

Make a dictionary! Print your name beside the letter it starts with. Think of words you know that start with other letters. Print them on the matching lines.

Tt

Uu

Vv

Ww

Xx

Yy

Zz

WEEK SEVEN

Day 5
MATH – 100 Chart

Fill in the missing numbers. Count aloud from 1 to 100.

1			4	5	6	7		9	10
11		13	14	15			18		
	22	23			26	27		29	
31		33	34		36		38		40
	42	43		45		47		49	
51			54	55			58		60
	62	63			66	67			
71			74	75			78	79	80
		83			86	87			90
91	92		94	95			98	99	

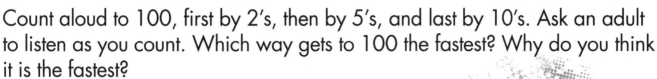

Day 5
MATH – Skip Counting

Count aloud to 100, first by 2's, then by 5's, and last by 10's. Ask an adult to listen as you count. Which way gets to 100 the fastest? Why do you think it is the fastest?

Count by 10's
Fill in the missing numbers in each row.

10 _____ 30 40 _____

30 40 _____ _____ 70

10 20 _____ _____ 50

60 70 80 _____ _____

Day 6
MATH – Before, After, and Between

Print the number that comes after.

23 __24__   41 _____   76 _____   33 _____

21 _____   39 _____   74 _____   31 _____

Print the number that comes before.

__92__ 93   _____ 46   _____ 23   _____ 33

_____ 90   _____ 44   _____ 21   _____ 30

Print the number that comes between.

15 __16__ 17   49 _____ 51   68 _____ 70

19 _____ 21   30 _____ 32   79 _____ 81

Print the numbers that come before and after.

__14__ 15 __16__   ___ 31 ___   ___ 59 ___

___ 40 ___   ___ 61 ___   ___ 99 ___

Day 6
MATH – Skip Counting

Count shoes by 2's.

__2__   _____   _____   _____   _____

_____   _____   _____   _____   _____

Count fingers by 5's.

__5__   _____   _____   _____   _____   _____   _____   _____   _____   _____

_____   _____   _____   _____   _____   _____   _____   _____   _____   _____

Count toes by 10's.

__10__   _____   _____   _____   _____   _____   _____   _____

_____   _____   _____   _____   _____   _____   _____   _____

Day 7
Review

Count the coins by 10's.

   10
_____

   _____

   _____

   _____

   _____

   _____

   _____

   _____

   _____

   _____

How many coins in all? _____

Day 7
Review

Print the colour words. Circle your favourite colour.

_____ red _____

_____

_____

_____

_____

_____

_____

_____

WEEK SEVEN

I Can Do It!
Put a checkmark beside each item you can do.

Day 1
I can spell colour words.. .... ❑

Day 2
I know how to unscramble words. .... ❑

Day 3
I know letters **Aa** to **Ll** .... ❑

Day 4
I know letters **Mm** to **Zz**.. .... ❑

Day 5
I can count to 100.. .... ❑

Day 6
I can skip count by 2's. .... ❑
I can skip count by 5's. .... ❑
I can skip count by 5's. .... ❑
I can skip count by 10's. .... ❑

Day 7
I did the review. .... ❑

Fresh Air Fun
Open a Toy Wash Service

To cool off on a hot day, how about offering a toy wash service? You will need water, cloths or sponges, three pails, and some towels. A tiny amount of liquid dish soap or other gentle soap is optional. Wear a bathing suit or clothes that you don't mind getting wet. Ask an adult to help you gather the right tools.

Gather toys that you want to wash. Make sure they are the kind that can get wet and soapy without being harmed. Ask an adult to make sure.

Fill one pail with water and a few drops of dish soap, and the other two with plain water. Put one pail containing water only aside. Spread out dry towels in a sunny spot where your toys will dry. Dip a cloth or sponge in the soapy water and wring it out. Wipe each toy all over with the soapy cloth. Then dip a clean cloth in the plain water, wring it out, and wipe each one with it to rinse off the soap. Set the toys on the dry towels to dry in the sunshine.

Then, cool yourself off after your hard work. Pick up the pail of plain water that you didn't use to wash or rinse with. Count down 10, 9, 8, 7, 6, 5, 4, 3, 2, 1…and…pour it over yourself!

Day 1
LANGUAGE – Alphabet Sequence

Say each letter. Print the uppercase letter that comes next.

A _B_____	**E** _____	**M** _____	**G** _____
Y _____	**P** _____	**D** _____	**H** _____
C _____	**L** _____	**U** _____	**K** _____
R _____	**F** _____	**O** _____	**I** _____

abc

Say each letter. Print the lowercase letter that comes next.

a _____	**e** _____	**m** _____	**g** _____
y _____	**p** _____	**d** _____	**h** _____
c _____	**l** _____	**u** _____	**k** _____
r _____	**f** _____	**o** _____	**i** _____

Day 1
MATH – Numbers to 20

Fill in the blanks with numbers to 20.

1				
6				
				20

Addition Facts

Collect counters (e.g. pebbles, beads, or beans). Use them to count the sums.

1 + 1 = ☐

3 + 2 = ☐

1 + 2 = ☐

1 + 4 = ☐

2 + 2 = ☐

2 + 3 = ☐

Day 2
MATH – Counting

Count. Circle the number.

(**1**) **2** **3**

5 **6** (**7**)

5 **6** **7**

8 **9** **10**

8 **9** **10**

1 **2** **3**

3 **4** **5**

3 **4** **5**

2 **3** **4**

8 **9** **10**

Day 2
MATH – Counting

Draw a line from the number to the matching set.

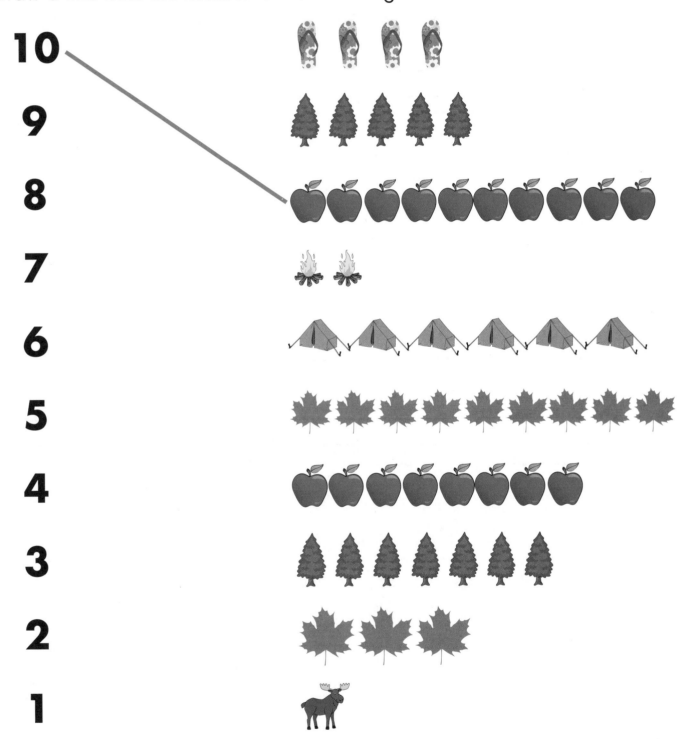

Day 3
SEASONS

There are four seasons in a year. Draw a picture to show each season. Write about something you like to do in each season.

In winter I _____
_____ .

In spring I _____
_____ .

Day 3
SEASONS

There are four seasons in a year. Draw a picture to show each season. Write about something you like to do in each season.

In summer I _____

_____.

In fall I _____

_____.

Day 4
WEATHER

Draw a line to connect each weather picture to the clothes you need.

What is the weather today? Draw the clothes you need today.

Day 4
CALENDAR – Printing the Days of the Week

There are seven days in a week. Point to each day and say the name aloud.

Sunday	Monday	Tuesday	Wednesday	Thursday	Friday	Saturday

Print the days.

Sunday

Monday

Tuesday

Wednesday

Thursday

Friday

Saturday

What day is today? _____

What day will tomorrow be? _____

Day 5
CALENDAR – Printing Months of the Year

Say each month aloud. Print each month. Remember that months always start with an uppercase letter!

January _____

February _____

March _____

April _____

May _____

June _____

July _____

August _____

September _____

October _____

November _____

December _____

My birthday is in _____.

Day 5
Days, Months, Seasons, Weather

Today's day is _____.
Today's month is _____.
The season is now _____.
Today the weather is _____.

🖐 FAMILY FUN ACTIVITY

Choose a calendar (or draw your own) to help your child keep track of the days, months, and weather over the summer. Point to today's date and talk about today's weather. Have your child draw pictures or use stickers to keep track of the weather each day. Point out special days coming up and ask your child to decorate those squares.

Day 6
MATH – Patterns

Identify the Core

(X Y Z) X Y Z X Y Z

These three letters repeat to create a pattern. Together they are called the core.

Circle the core of each pattern.

Day 6
MATH – Patterns

Draw the shapes that continue the patterns.

Spy Spy Spy _____ _____ _____

Growing Patterns
Continue the growing number patterns on the lily pads.

4

2

3 6

5 10

Day 7
MATH – Patterns

Use crayons of different colours to draw your own patterns.

Draw a pattern using different shapes.

Draw a pattern using different colours.

Draw a pattern using different sizes.

Day 7
MATH – Addition and Subtraction

Count and add.

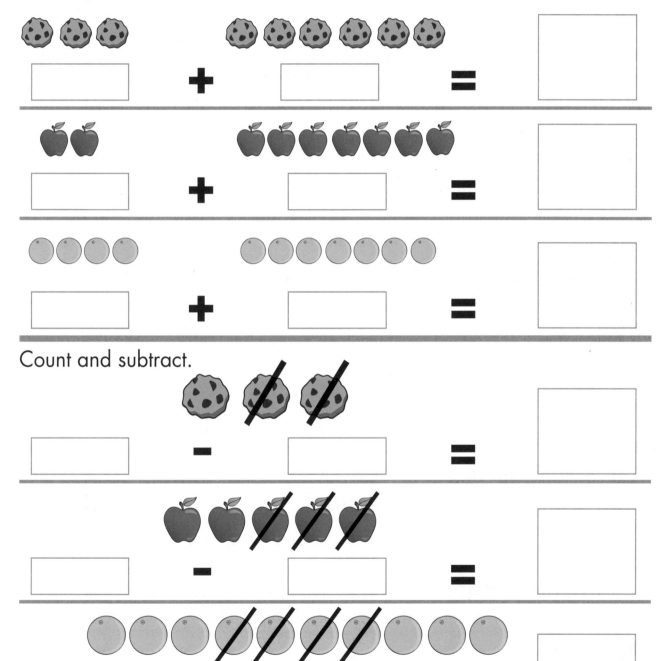

Count and subtract.

I Can Do It!
Put a checkmark beside each item you can do.

Day 1
I know upper- and lowercase letters. .... ❑
I can can print numbers to 20. .... ❑
I can add to 5. .... ❑

Day 2
I can count and match to 10. .... ❑

Day 3
I know about seasons. .... ❑

Day 4
I know about weather. .... ❑
I can print the days of the week. .... ❑

Day 5
I can print the months. .... ❑
I know today's day, month, season. .... ❑

Day 6
I know about patterns. .... ❑

Day 7
I can make my own patterns. .... ❑
I can use counting to add and subtract .... ❑

Fresh Air Fun
Changing Seasons

Have fun outside! Find something outside that looks different in each season, for example, a tree or bush or flower. How does it look now? How will it change in fall, winter, and spring? Will you be able to see it during the winter? Draw pictures to show how it changes in each season.

Day 1
LANGUAGE – Letter Sounds

Say the name of each picture. Draw a line to the letter that makes the beginning sound.

Day 1
LANGUAGE – Letter Sound

Draw a line each from letter to a picture of something that starts with that sound.

Day 2
MATH – Counting and Matching to 20

Count the pictures. Circle the matching number.
Hint: Put an X on each thing as you count. One has been started for you.

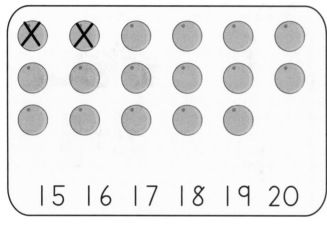

15   16   17   18   19   20

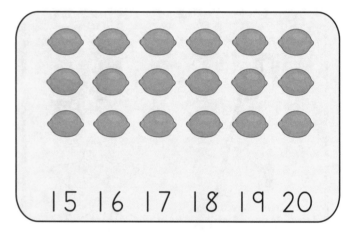

15   16   17   18   19   20

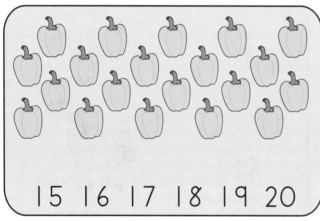

15   16   17   18   19   20

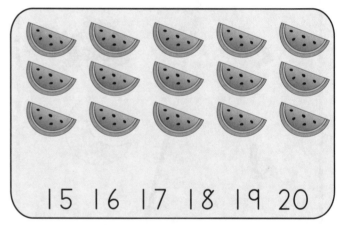

15   16   17   18   19   20

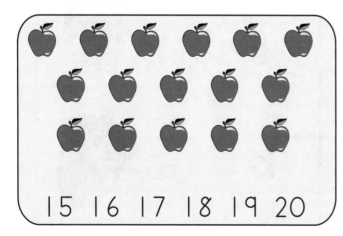

15   16   17   18   19   20

15   16   17   18   19   20

Day 2
MATH – Counting and Adding to 20
Trace the number. Count the dots. Add dots to make the number.

Day 3
LANGUAGE – Colour Words
Trace the colour word. Colour the crayon to match.

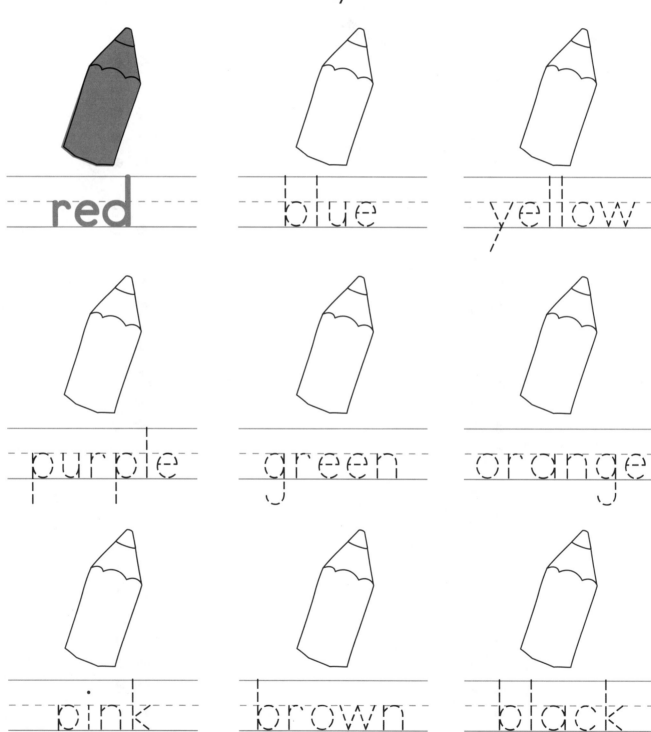

Day 3
LANGUAGE – Colour Words
Colour each balloon to match the word.

Day 4
MATH – Measurement

How many squares tall is each tree? Count the squares. Print the number.

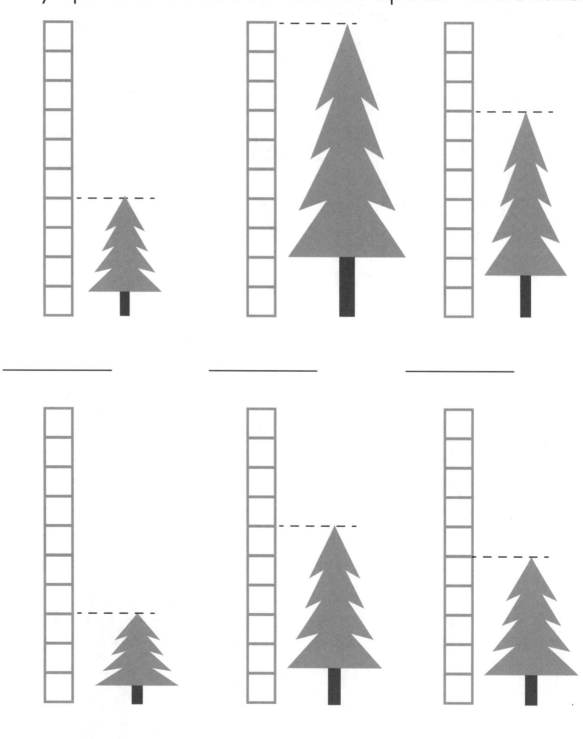

Day 4
MATH – Measurement

Ask an adult to cut a piece of string as long as your arm. Use the string to measure things at home. Find things that are shorter than the string, the same length as the string, and longer than the string. Draw pictures of what you find.

Shorter than the String

Same Length as the String

Longer than the String

Day 5
MATH – Comparing More and Less

Count items in each set. Print the number in the box. Compare each pair.
Circle the set that has **more**.

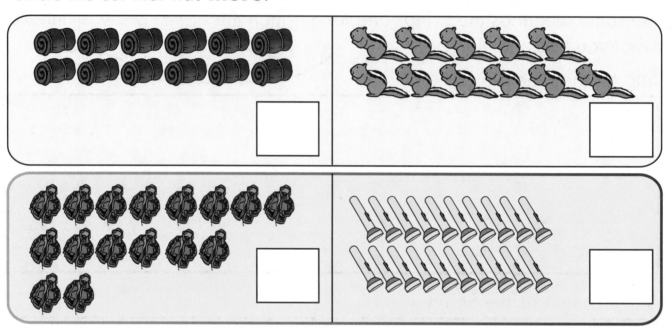

Count items in each set. Print the number in the box. Compare each pair.
Circle the set that has **less**.

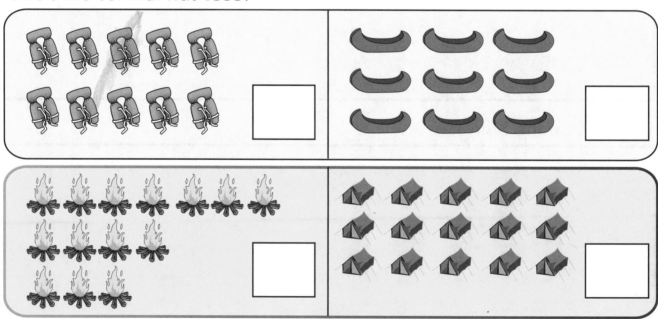

Day 5
MATH – Comparing and Crossing Out to Match Numbers

How many items are in each set? Compare each pair. Cross out items to make each pair of sets the **same**.

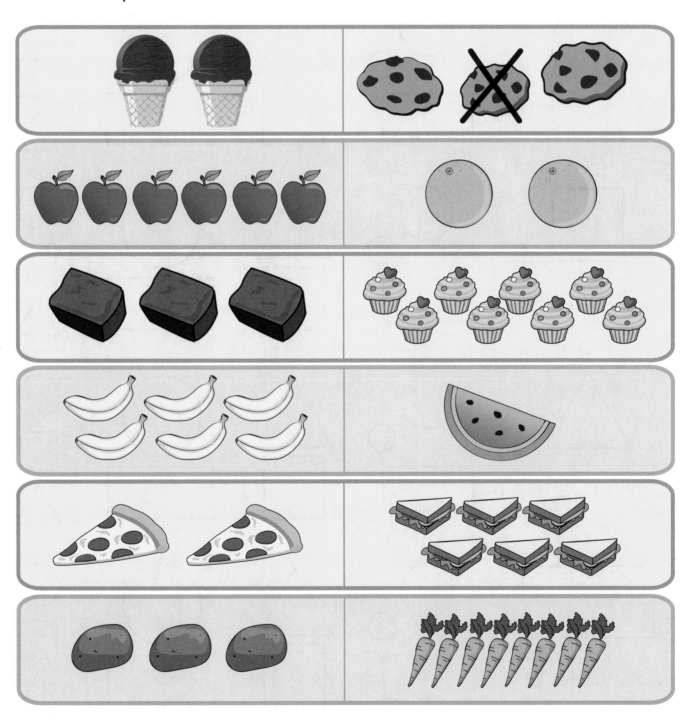

Day 6
MATH – Shapes and Shape Words

Trace the shape words. Colour the shapes that belong in each family.

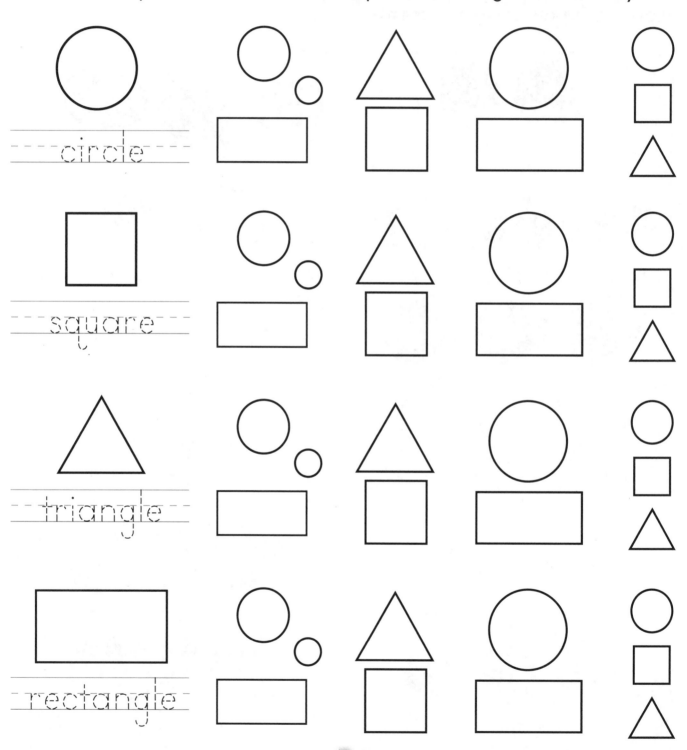

circle

square

triangle

rectangle

Day 6
MATH – Shapes and Shape Words

Trace the shape words. Colour the shapes that belong in each family.

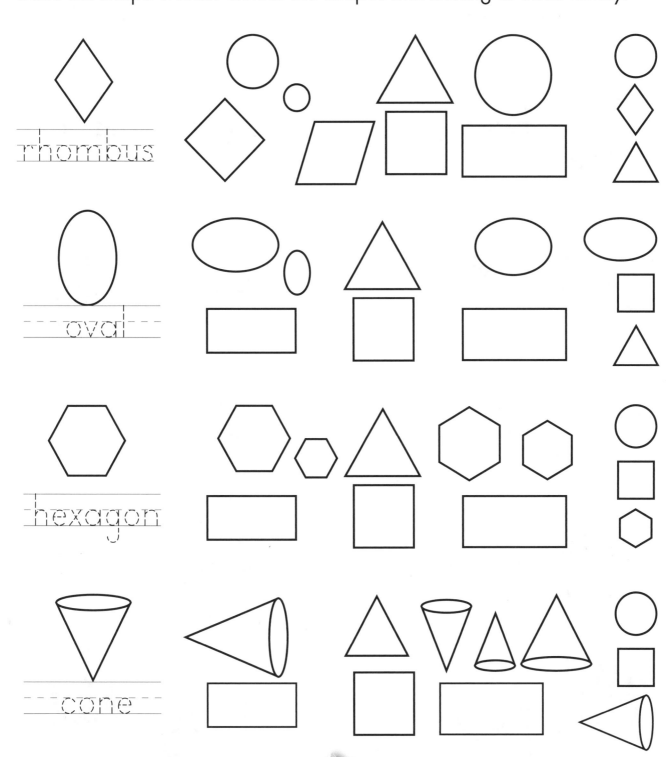

Day 7
LANGUAGE – Short Vowel Sounds

Look at each picture. Read each word. Draw lines to connect words that have the same sort vowel sound.

 fan

tent

 net

cat

 fish

pig

stop

sun

 pup

frog

Day 7
LANGUAGE – Rhyming Words
Look at each picture. Read each word. Draw lines to connect words that rhyme.

 pan

pen

 hen

man

 sip

hop

 top

bun

 sun

lip

WEEK NINE

I Can Do It!
Put a checkmark beside each item you can do.

Day 1
I know upper- and lowercase letters. .... ❑
I can identify beginning letter sounds....................... ❑

Day 2
I can count and match quantities to numbers up to 20. . ❑

Day 3
I can trace and read colour words. .... ❑

Day 4
I can measure height using squares. .... ❑
I can measure length using string. .... ❑

Day 5
I can count and compare more and less.................... ❑
I can compare quantities and cross out to make
them match. .... ❑

Day 6
I can trace shape words and identify some 2-D shapes. ❑
I can identify one 3-D shape................................ ❑

Day 7
I can match short vowel sounds............................. ❑
I can match rhyming words. .... ❑

WEEK NINE

Fresh Air Fun
Measuring with Shoes

Have fun outside! Use your shoes to measure things outdoors. You will need your shoes, paper, and pencil.

First, look around for these things: one sidewalk square, one bike, one sandbox, and one fence. If you don't find all of those things, think of other things to measure. Make a list of the four things you will measure.

Start with the sidewalk square first. Stand at one end of the square with your heels right against the edge. That is one shoe length. Take one step forward, putting your foot down so that your heel touches the toes of your other foot. That makes two shoe lengths. Continue in that way until you come to the other edge of the sidewalk square. When your foot goes over the end of the sidewalk square, finish counting. Write the number down on your list. How many shoe lengths is the sidewalk square? If you wore adult shoes while you measured, would the number be bigger or smaller? Why?

Measure the other things on your list in the same way.

Day 1
LANGUAGE – Sight Words

Sight words help you read and write stories.
Print each word. Draw a line to the matching word.
Look for these words in a book or magazine. How many can you find?

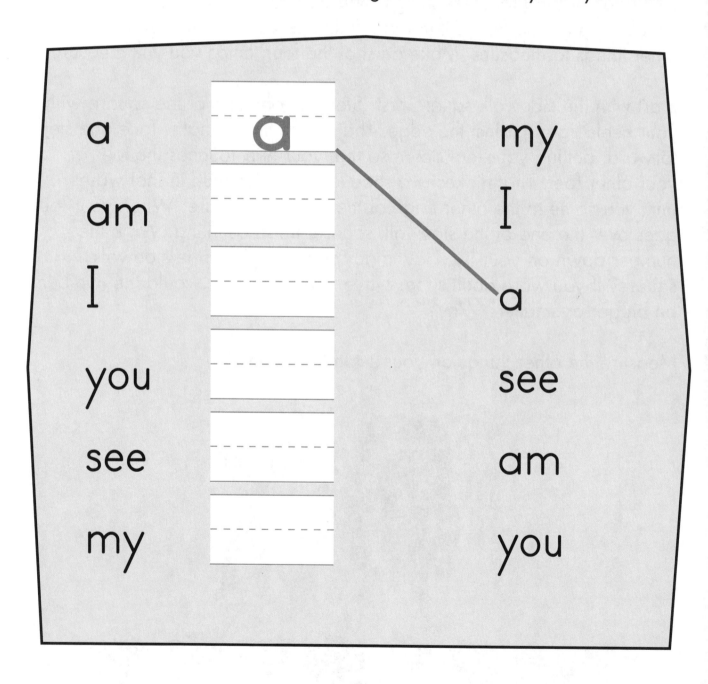

a

am

I

you

see

my

a

my

I

a

see

am

you

Day 1
MATH – Telling Time

Colour the big minute hand red.
Colour the little hour hand green. Trace the numbers.
What number does the little hand point to? That tells the hour.

This clock says

_____ o'clock.

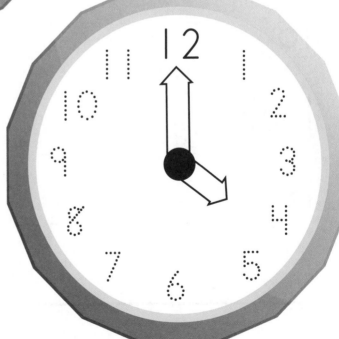

This clock says

_____ o'clock.

Day 2
LANGUAGE – Sight Words

Sight words help you read and write stories.
Print each word. Draw a line to the matching word.
Look for these words in a book or magazine. How many can you find?

	and	is
and		
at		me
me		look
to		at
look		and
is		to

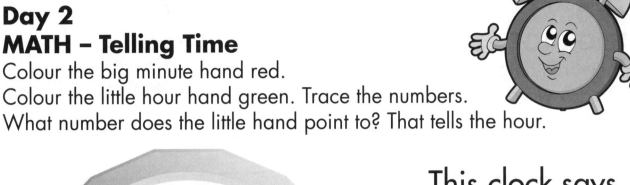

Day 2
MATH – Telling Time
Colour the big minute hand red.
Colour the little hour hand green. Trace the numbers.
What number does the little hand point to? That tells the hour.

This clock says

_____ o'clock.

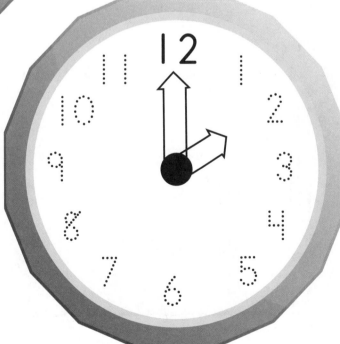

This clock says

_____ o'clock.

Day 3
LANGUAGE – Sight Words

Sight words help you read and write stories.
Print each word. Draw a line to the matching word.
Look for these words in a book or magazine. How many can you find?

can	**can**	Dad
Dad		can
he		it
in		like
it		he
like		in

Day 3
MATH – Money

nickel	dime	quarter	dollar	two dollar
5¢	10¢	25¢	(loonie) $1.00	(toonie) $2.00

Draw a line from the coin to its value.

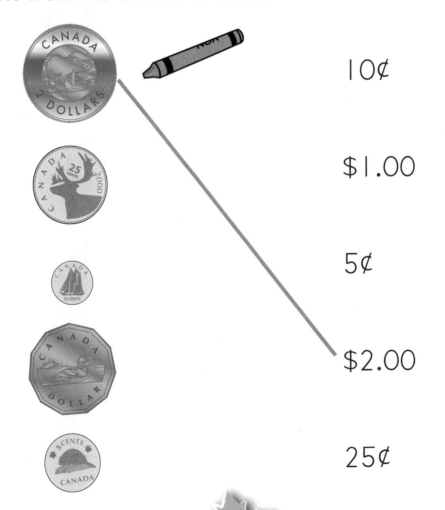

10¢

$1.00

5¢

$2.00

25¢

Day 4
LANGUAGE – Sight Words

Sight words help you read and write stories.
Print each word. Draw a line to the matching word.
Look for these words in a book or magazine. How many can you find?

	you	at
you		you
am		am
at		day
be		be
by		by
day		

Day 4
MATH – Comparing Heavier and Lighter

Find these items at home.

Heavier   Lighter

Which is heavier? Draw a blue circle ○. Which is lighter? Draw a green circle ○.

Day 5
LANGUAGE – Sight Words

Sight words help you read and write stories.
Print each word. Draw a line to the matching word.
Look for these words in a book or magazine. How many can you find?

ran	ran	say
say		ran
up		who
who		up
why		when
when		why

Day 5
MATH – Addition with Counters
Count. Print the numbers.
How many all together. Print the numbers.

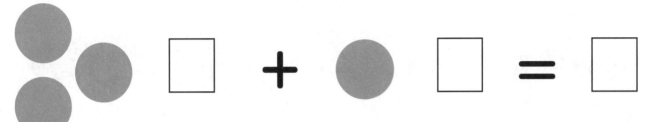

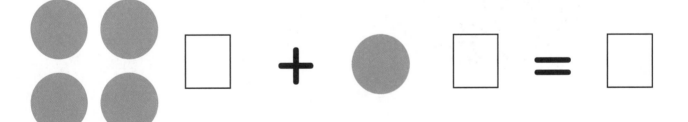

Day 6
LANGUAGE – Printing Sentences

Read each sentence. Print each sentence.

I like to run with my dog.

The bird flies in the sky.

Day 6
MATH – Subtraction

Count. Print the number in the first box. Subtract 1 by crossing off shapes. How many left? Print that number in the last box.

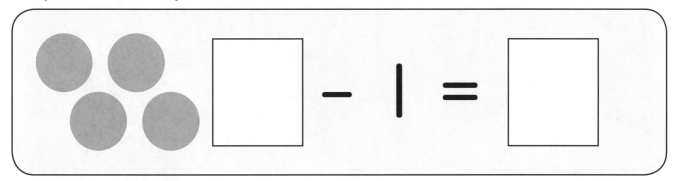

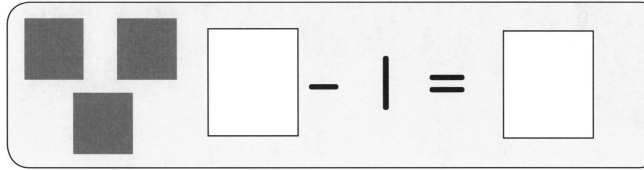

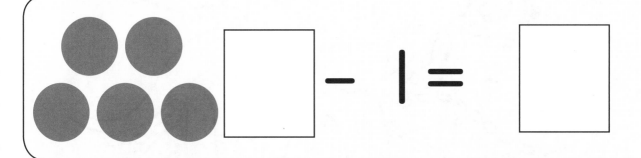

Day 7
Language - Alphabetical Order
Connect the dots from a to z. Colour the picture.

Day 7
MATH - Counting

Connect the dots from 1 to 25. Colour the picture.

WEEK TEN

I Can Do It!
Put a checkmark beside each item you can do.

Day 1
I can print and match six sight words........................ ❑
I can tell the hour on a clock................................. ❑

Day 2
I can print and match six more sight words................. ❑
I can tell the hour on a clock................................. ❑

Day 3
I can print and match six more sight words................. ❑
I can match coins with their value............................ ❑

Day 4
I can print and match six more sight words................. ❑
I can compare heavier and lighter........................... ❑

Day 5
I can print and match six more sight words................. ❑
I can add to 5 with counters. .... ❑

Day 6
I can trace and print sentences. .... ❑
I can subtract 1 using counters.............................. ❑

Day 7
I can connect the dots in alphabetical order................ ❑
I can connect the dots in number order from 1 to 25. ... ❑

Fresh Air Fun
Build a Volcano

Have fun outside! Build your own erupting volcano. You will need some sand or garden soil, a stick or small shovel, about 15 ml (1 Tbs.) baking soda, and 250 ml (1 cup) or more of vinegar.

First, build a mound of garden soil or sand about 30 cm high. Then, using a stick or small shovel, make a deep hole in the middle. Sprinkle the baking soda into the hole. Last, slowly pour the vinegar into the hole. Watch your volcano erupt!

Draw a picture of your volcano erupting.

DIPLOMA

This certificate of completion presented to

_____

Print your name on the line.

You did it!

Congratulations on completing *Super Summer Learning Kindergarten to Grade 1.*
You are all ready for next year!

PHONICS FLASH CARDS CUT-OUT

Sample
Have a parent carefully cut cards out along solid line.

Tape or glue the sides together.

Fold along dotted line

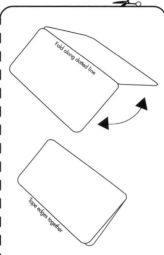

Fold along dotted line

Tape edges together

at

bat
cat
hat
cats
chat
batter

ate

date
hate
late
mate
crater
plate

an

and
can
man
pan
plan
stand

ane

cane
lane
mane
pane
crane
plane

ain

gain
main
rain
brain
stain
train

PHONICS FLASH CARDS

ap

cap
gap
lap
map
trap
strap

ape

cape
gape
nape
tape
drape
shape

en

den
hen
pen
ten
then
blend

ee

keep
green
sheep
steep
sweep
cheerful

et

get
let
met
wet
yet
better

ed

bed
red
led
shed
batted
petted

PHONICS FLASH CARDS

ell

bell
fell
sell
tell
shell
telling

ight

light
might
night
right
sight
flight

old

bold
cold
fold
folded
holding
told

ow

bow
cow
how
owl
chow
towel

ea

eat
bean
hear
seat
treat
eating

ut

but
cut
rut
shut
strut
butter

PHONICS FLASH CARDS

ute

cute
jute
lute
mute
brute
flute

ot

got
hot
lot
not
blot
shot

oa

boat
coat
goal
goat
road
toad

oo

door
foot
soot
wood
wool
floor

oo

boot
fool
hoot
loot
root
cooler

in

bin
win
chin
shin
wind
winner

PHONICS FLASH CARDS

ine

mine
nine
pine
vine
shine
diner

it

bit
hit
pit
sit
quit
hitter

ite

bite
kite
quite
biter
polite
write

y

by
my
dry
fry
shy
trying

ch

chat
chap
chip
chin
chum
much

sh

shed
shin
ship
dish
wash
splashing

th

that
the
them
then
this
rather

th

thick
thin
think
bath
path
math

qu

quick
quill
quip
quit
quiz
quilt

cl

clap
clay
cliff
cloud
clown
uncle

cr

cry
crab
crib
crash
crowd
across

ing

ring
bring
thing
finger
string
singing

PHONICS FLASH CARDS

er

fern
germ
perk
singer
hotter
quicker

est

best
nest
pest
test
pester
biggest

ar

bar
car
far
dark
park
part
star

ir

air
sir
bird
girl
chirp
circle

ore

bore
chore
more
pore
sore
tore

ur

fur
blur
hurt
purr
turn
burst

PHONICS FLASH CARDS

ay

bay
day
say
clay
pray
stray

st

stab
stand
stew
stick
sting
stop

tr

trap
trim
trip
track
trick
truck

str

strap
straw
stray
strip
string
strong

un

bun
fun
sun
under
untie
until

all

ball
call
fall
mall
tall
stall

PHONICS FLASH CARDS

bl

blot
able
black
blast
blend
marble

sl

slap
slim
slip
slop
asleep
sliver

dr

drip
drop
dress
drill
drink
address

ou

found
hound
mound
pound
round
around

gr

grab
gram
grit
grass
ground
agree

Make your own flash cards!

COUNTING FLASH CARDS CUT-OUT

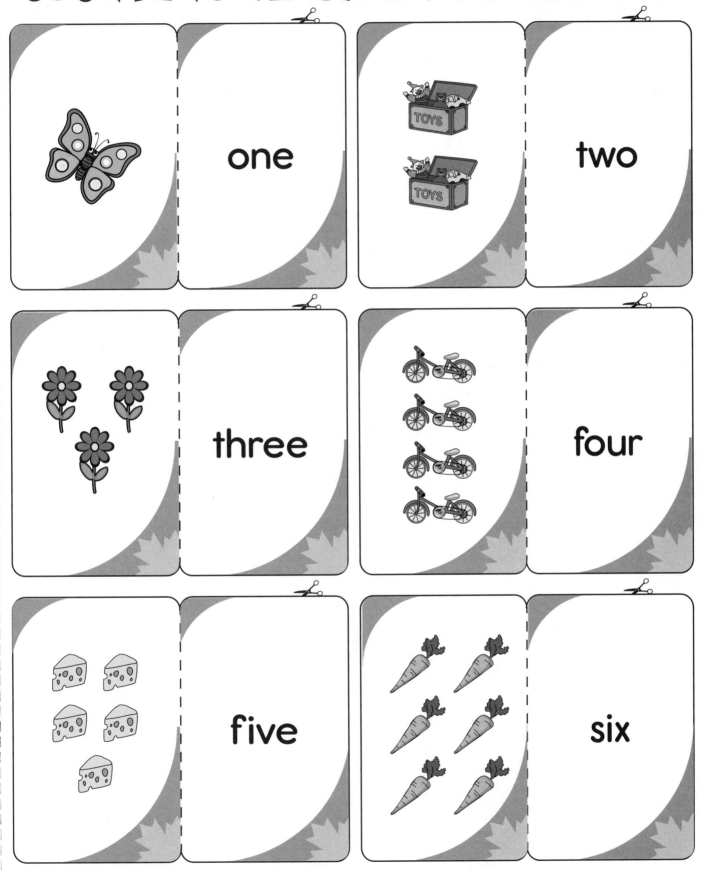

one

two

three

four

five

six

COUNTING FLASH CARDS

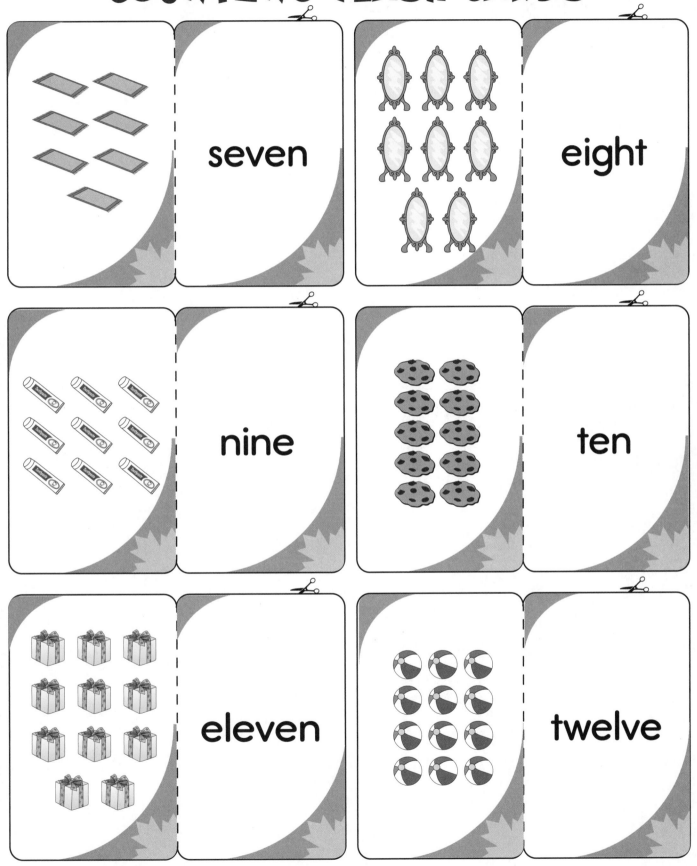

seven

eight

nine

ten

eleven

twelve

181

COUNTING FLASH CARDS

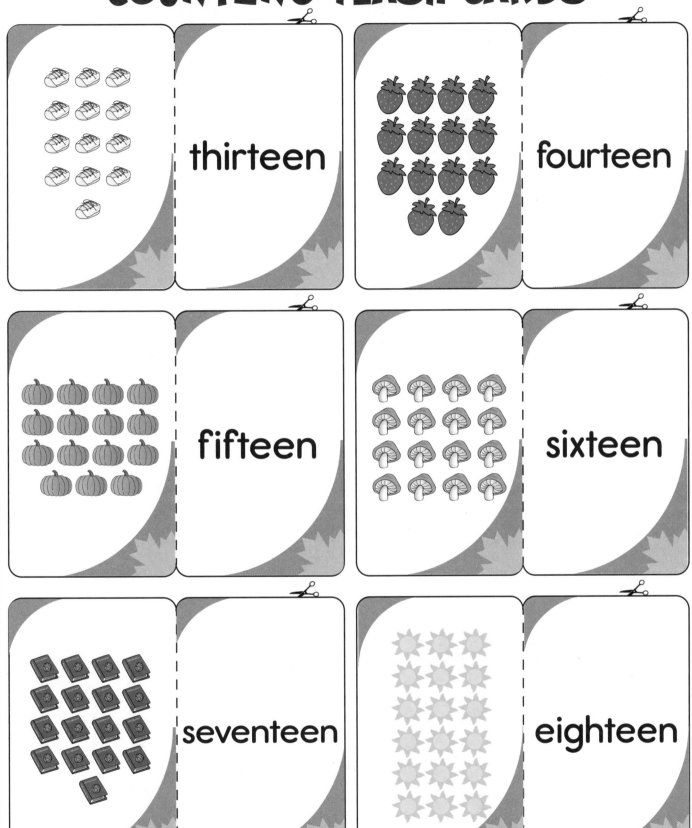

thirteen

fourteen

fifteen

sixteen

seventeen

eighteen

COUNTING FLASH CARDS

nineteen

twenty

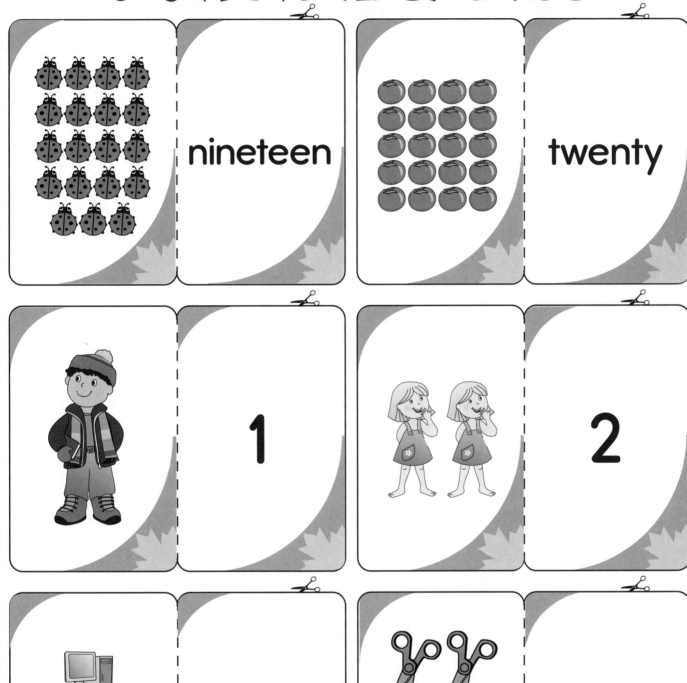

1

2

3

4

COUNTING FLASH CARDS

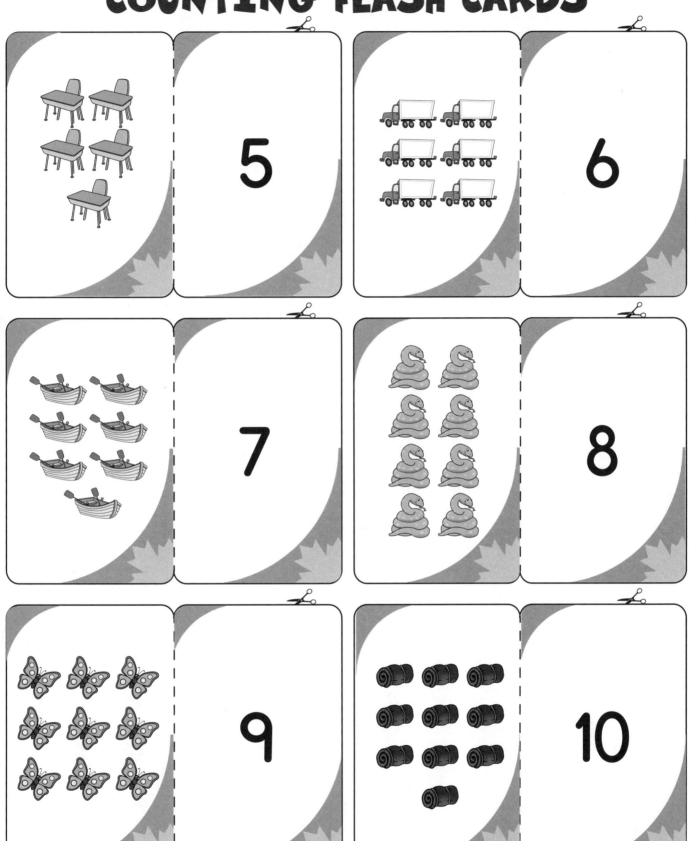

COUNTING FLASH CARDS

11

12

13

14

15

16

COUNTING FLASH CARDS

17

18

19

20

Make your own flash cards!